THE COD

Hauling in a heavy catch of cod close to the shore of St. John's, Newfoundland. (Department of Fisheries of Canada)

THE COD

Albert C. Jensen

Thomas Y. Crowell Company

NEW YORK

ESTABLISHED 1834

C. P. Idyll, Editor

To my wife, Pat,

and to the memory of my mother

Acknowledgments

PEOPLE IN MANY FIELDS have been generous in giving help while I was writing this book. I am deeply grateful to my wife for her patience during the long months while the book was being prepared. Her suggestions and corrections in the manuscript were invaluable. Special thanks go to Dr. C. P. Idyll, Chairman of the Division of Fishery Sciences, Rosenstiel School of Marine and Atmospheric Sciences, University of Miami, Florida, for his advice and guidance throughout the project. Robert K. Brigham, National Marine Fisheries Service Biological Laboratory, Woods Hole, Massachusetts, was a valuable consultant on photographs. Many of the photographs used here were taken by him. Additional photographs were made available through the courtesy of the Plymouth Cordage Division, Columbian Rope Company, Auburn, New York. Finally, I must express my sincerest thanks to Barbara H. Durciansky for painstaking preparation of the manuscript. Her forbearance through the several revisions helped sustain the effort.

Contents

1 The Codfish, Man, and History   1
2 The Cod in Legend and Custom   9
3 Natural History of the Cod   21
4 The Varieties of Cod   37
5 The Beef of the Sea   51
6 Development of the World Cod Fishery   67
7 Cod and the Discovery of America   81
8 Codfish, Rum, and Slaves   93
9 Lone Men in Frail Dories   109
10 Trawlermen and Anglers   127
11 The North Atlantic Cod Fishery Today   143
12 Conservation of the Cod   155
    Selected Bibliography   174
    Index   175

A lone doryman hastens back to his schooner just before fog closes in. Below, the Gertrude L. Thebaud, *launched in 1930, the last in a long line of Gloucester dory schooners with tall spars, topmast, and bowsprit. (Columbian Rope Company, Gorton Corporation)*

1

The Codfish, Man, and History

SINCE BEFORE THE BEGINNINGS of written history, one fish above all others has had profound effect on the social and economic structure of the peoples of North America and Europe.

This simple fish, the Atlantic cod, today occupies an important place in world fisheries landings. It has also long occupied an important place in man's cultural and economic activities. For centuries it has been a symbol of the wealth of the sea. It early became an integral part of the traditions of Christianity and later became an element in the degrading U.S. slave trade. It was the source of great personal wealth for a few, and was a common food for the masses. Shakespeare wrote about it in his plays, using it as a term of loathing and repugnance. It supplied the Vikings and other sea rovers with food during their explorations and figured prominently in the negotiations for the treaty that ended the American War of Independence. And, indirectly, the cod contributed to the extinction of the great auk, a large, flightless North Atlantic bird whose flocks once numbered in the millions.

Throughout the centuries, man tried to learn more about the cod, to understand its comings and goings, its increases and scarcity. The cod and its fellow dweller of the cold northern seas, the herring, are bound in a complex socio-economic fabric woven by man. It is to man's benefit to know and understand everything possible about the cod. But, curiously, men cannot even agree on how the fish got its common name. An etymological argument traces the word cod to the short stick on which the ancients stretched the split fish for drying in the sun. The argument starts with the Latin name *gadus* used by the Romans, who derived it from the Sanskrit root, *cad*, or *gad*, meaning a rod. The same root later came into English in "goad" and, perhaps, cat [gad]-o-nine-tails. The Anglo-Saxons called the fish "cod," from the word *gad* or *goad*, meaning a stick. This same derivation appears, for example, in the German word for cod, *stockfisch*, from *stock*, a stick.

The values and attributes men associate with the cod have remained with us, with some minor changes, through the centuries. Thus the ancient benefits of the cod have a place even now in the twentieth century. In July 1971, the National Marine Fisheries Service announced from Washington, D.C., "The codfish, famous as a major item of commerce and trade, in colonial America, has quietly re-emerged as a sought after item in the modern marketplace." This may be true for the marketplace in the United States, but in the other nations bordering the North Atlantic, the cod had never left the market but has reigned high among fishes for more than a thousand years.

Forty-eight fish species are considered commercially important in the North Atlantic. Cod heads the list in the amount landed, followed by herring, and both species have had a long historical relationship. Over the centuries, the markets of Europe, Canada, Greenland, and Iceland have seen a veritable flood of codfish taken from the cold northern waters. John P. Wise, Woods Hole fishery biologist, calculated the 1957 catch of cod in the Atlantic to be nearly 13 billion pounds per year. "Conservatively," he said, "these figures represent over one thousand million individual fish landed with a value to fishermen of about $200 million." He goes on to state that so important is the cod to our modern world fisheries, and so great is the demand for this fish that about 10 per cent by weight of all the world's fishery products is Atlantic cod. In 1970, it amounted to a total of nearly 7 billion pounds, enough to supply four servings to every man, woman, and child in the world. The U.S. share of this catch was 53 million pounds.

Consumer demand for cod has gone through a cycle in the past century. In the mid-1920's, the housewives turned away from dried salt cod, commonly available up to that time, looking for fish that were easier to prepare. It was soon eclipsed by other species, especially haddock and flounder. But now, a half century later, cod has come into its own as the very thing the housewife is looking for—a convenience

[2]

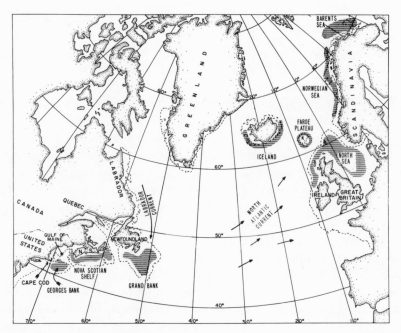

The major cod-fishing grounds of the North Atlantic. (*National Marine Fisheries Service*)

food. Precooked codfish sticks were introduced in the 1950's (in England, they are called "fish fingers"), and then "fish portions" appeared on the market, particularly in prepared and cooked "TV dinners." Today, major users of cod are the franchised fish-and-chips shops, with their appeal of "fast food—eat it here or take it home." The fish-and-chips franchise business is recognized by the U.S. Department of Commerce as possibly the most rapidly developing market segment for fishery products. It began with a single outlet on the West Coast in 1965, growing to more than a thousand by January 1971, and now uses an estimated 30 to 60 million pounds of fishery products each year. Since its beginning, this industry has almost exclusively used cod.

Recreational fisherman also eagerly seek the cod although its fighting ability at the end of a line is said to be about the same as an old rubber boot. The zeal of the cod fisherman is intense and if the fishing is good the reward will be a gunny sack or two filled with 100 pounds of cod. The hope of each angler is to top the world-record cod that weighed over ninety-eight pounds.

Dr. Robert Cushman Murphy, Curator Emeritus of the American

Museum of Natural History, once remarked, "The Spaniards came to the New World for gold, but the Portuguese, English, and French came for codfish. The value of the codfish has lasted longer than the gold of the Indies." And so it has. Each year, as they have for nearly five centuries, fishermen from many nations brave the stormy crossing of the North Atlantic to fish for cod off Newfoundland. Today, some twenty nations are represented in these vast codfishing fleets.

What is so special about this fish? The basic reasons behind its popularity are quite simple. It is abundant. It grows to large size. Its almost bland flesh is nutritious and lends itself to a variety of cooking methods. And, finally, it is well adapted to salting and drying, an important consideration even in this day of space travel and other modern miracles.

The Atlantic cod (*Gadus morhua*, Linnaeus) is the type fish of a large family of fishes called the Gadidae that includes the haddock, the pollock, and the hake. Cod are found on both sides of the North Atlantic from the northern Barents Sea south to the Bay of Biscay, around Iceland and the southern tip of Greenland, all the way down to North Carolina. They usually live near the ocean floor and have been caught in water as shallow as six feet and as deep as 1,500 feet. Many cod are found near shore over rough bottom, but the most famous cod grounds are the offshore banks such as the Grand Bank of Newfoundland, Georges Bank, and those around the Faroe Islands and the Lofoten Islands.

The cod could be described as a typical fish. It has a streamlined shape with three dorsal fins, a broad tail, and a small barbel, a whisker-like taste organ under the lower jaw. Its color ranges from gray or gray-green to brick red to almost black. The upper parts are liberally marked with spots, and there is a prominent light lateral line.

Cod are winter spawners and each female sheds between 3 and 9 million eggs, depending on the size of the fish. Only one or two eggs out of each of the millions from each female survive to adulthood. The pelagic eggs hatch in about two to three weeks and develop into grotesque-looking larvae that feed on plankton, the tiny drifting organisms of the sea. Later, when the young cod are about three or four inches long, they descend to the ocean depths to live on the bottom. The adults feed mostly on invertebrates (clams, mussels, crabs, squid) and small fish. But many nonfood items have been found in their stomachs, including boots, cans, bits of wood, and even a set of false teeth.

[4]

Biologists studying the scales and otoliths of cod find that it is a rela-tively fast-growing fish and lives to be at least twenty-two years old. It is possible for them to live for a half century if they do not fall victim to accidents, disease, large sharks, or fishermen.

Its high-quality white flesh has been in demand as food from prehis-toric times. Split, salted, and dried cod flesh can be kept for months without spoiling, even in tropical climates. Salt cod was often a stan-dard provision aboard sailing ships and became known as "beef of the sea." Viking explorers carried dried cod aboard their dragon ships when they explored the New World, as did many later sea adventur-ers. Some modern historians claim that the Pilgrim fathers were moti-vated by a desire not only to worship as they pleased but to exploit the rich cod resources that Captain John Smith, Bartholomew Gosnold, and others had found off the New England coast.

The relationship between fish and religion is a very ancient one, and the cod has figured prominently in this regard. The connection is par-ticularly strong in the Judeo-Christian tradition. Drs. E. R. Pariser and O. A. Hammerle, of the National Marine Fisheries Service, report: "In Jewish tradition . . . the pious were fish living in the water of the Torah." This concept was brought over into Christianity. "Fish was frequently represented in the West as a substitute for wine in the scene of the Last Supper. The earliest of such scenes exists in the catacombs of St. Callistus, Rome," according to Pariser and Hammerle.

The consumption of fish as a religious practice assumed great impor-tance in Europe from the eighth century onward, when the Church of Rome allowed the use of fish on Friday. Prior to this, Friday was a rig-idly observed fast day and not even fish could be eaten. Dried salt cod and salt herring quickly became the prime fast-day foods, especially during the springtime season of Lent. But economics soon obscured the religious issue, and the observance of fish days and Lent in England during the latter half of the sixteenth century was enforced largely be-cause of a scarcity of red meat. What meat there was went to feed the men of the British Navy who were mustered to oppose Philip of Spain. Some claim that the objectives of fish days were largely secular rather than sacred, to stimulate fishing and ship building. The fishing fleets were looked on as providing training for men before they went into the navy, then so very important to the economic and political well-being of most of Europe.

In North America, the domestic cod fishery developed slowly, first as a subsistence fishery, then as a full-blown industry whose products were widely sold abroad. The life of the fisherman was hard and cruel and so was the life of the families they left ashore. Sudden winter storms on the offshore banks often decimated the fleets and brought disaster to the home ports. One such storm, a two-day gale on Georges Bank, in February 1879, sank thirteen schooners and drowned 143 fishermen from Gloucester, Massachusetts. In 1883, seventeen vessels and 209 fishermen from Gloucester went down in gales and other storms on the banks. Forty of the men left widows and a total of sixty-eight fatherless children. In addition to the drownings, seventy-one fishermen either capsized in their frail dories and were rescued, or drifted off in fog but luckily were able to row to a landfall more than fifty miles away.

The early fishermen were plagued by other problems, not the least of which was finding proper bait for their hooks. When squid or herring were not available, they used whatever came to hand, including the sea birds that flocked about the vessels. The dorymen tossed bits of cod liver on the water to attract the birds and then fished for them with handlines and small hooks baited with cod liver. When a bird was caught, the fisherman pulled it to him, held it under one arm, and crushed its skull with his teeth to kill it. Both the entrails and the flesh were used as cod bait. Frequently the fishy-tasting birds were served aboard ship in pot pies and stews to supplement the monotonous diet of fish and salt beef.

Hagdons (*Puffinus major* and *P. fuligninosus*) as well as gulls (*Larus* sp.) were taken in what the dorymen called "hag fishing." But the practice, which had been introduced to fill the void caused by the disappearance of the great auk (*Pinguinus impennis*), died out after about 1875.

The great auk was the only flightless bird of North America. It was a large bird, about thirty inches tall, and resembled a penguin, although it was related to the puffin. Like the penguin, it was awkward on land but in the water it was a graceful and marvelously efficient bird. Each year the flocks swam 3,000 miles from their wintering grounds on the Outer Banks of North Carolina to nesting sites on rocky islands around Iceland, Greenland, and Newfoundland. During its feeding forays it would descend 200 feet and swim underwater for half a mile in search of small herring, crabs, and other prey. The auks' enemies were large sharks and killer whales, but these only made small inroads on the flocks of millions of the large birds. Because the auk was so abundant, cod fishermen on their way from Europe to the Grand Bank stopped at the barren nesting islands to feast on fresh auk meat and to salt down the flesh for bait. Later, a trade in auk flesh and feathers developed in Europe.

Richard Whitbourn, an early seventeenth-century writer, described the great auks as "penguins, bigge as Geese, and flie not. They multiply so infinitely upon a certain flat Island that men drive them from thence upon a board into their Boates, hundreds at a time, as if God had made the innocencie of so poore a creature to become an admirable instrument for the sustenation of man."

The men herded the birds together on the islands, clubbed them to death, and loaded the carcasses into the boats. They also shot them from their boats with scatter guns loaded with bits of scrap iron, old bent nails, pieces of chain, and lead balls. And, in an inspiration of destruction, the birds were herded—as Whitbourn described it—toward the boats in the surf so that the men would not have far to carry the carcasses. Then the auks were forced to walk a plank from the shore and across the gunwales where waiting men with clubs crushed the birds' skulls and tumbled the carcasses into the boat.

No population of animals can stand such intense exploitation for very long. Since the auk mated for life and the females laid only one egg each year, reproduction was unable to keep up with the numbers killed. Soon the flocks of millions became flocks of thousands and finally it became evident that the auk was very scarce indeed. Museums and private collectors began a race to see who could get skins of the great auk before the birds disappeared from the face of the earth. On June 3, 1844, the last great auk was killed by collectors on Eldey Island, ten miles west of Iceland.

It is safe to say that no one learned any lesson when the great auk became extinct. Our record of exploiting natural resources makes this painfully evident. But what of the codfish? Are we to apply any rational management to the exploitation of that bountiful resource? It is clear that the sea and its fishes will have to supply more of our food than is presently done. It is fortunate, too, that for the codfish, at least, we have available a vast body of literature and experience on which to base schemes for wise use of the resource. What is needed more than anything else is the determination to put the knowledge and experience to work for man's benefit.

Two classic scenes from the era of Kipling's Captains Courageous: *Cutting bait aboard a cod schooner and, below, baiting the individual hooks of the trawl.* (Columbian Rope Company)

2

The Cod in Legend and Custom

FOR CENTURIES THE COD was such an everyday commodity that it was inevitable that its name should pass into the language in a variety of ways. The fish was held in such high regard that representations of cod were used on documents, coins, legal papers, home ornamentations, and in the chambers of legislative bodies. It was simultaneously a symbol of wealth and an epithet to describe the clumsiest of louts.

As a food, the cod was commonplace, but like many a homely acquaintance it occupied an honored place in the affections of humble people.

As a symbol the cod shared an honored place with other fishes. The figure of a fish has always been a powerful symbol. A fish was one of the first (if not the very first) symbol of Christ used by the early Christians. This derives from the Greek word for fish, IXΘΥΣ, whose letters are the initials of the phrase Jesus Christ, Son of God, Savior. Christians harried in the Roman world and forced to carry on their pursuits in secret left signs to each other in the form of a crudely drawn fish. Fish are very prominent as a sacred symbol in the painting and sculpture of the ancient Church, and they are used as devices on Church signet rings and seals. A Spanish dictionary of symbols explains that two attributes of the fish give rise to its widespread use as an emblem. First, its bobbinlike shape makes it a sort of "bird of the nether regions," symbolic of sacrifice and of the relationship between heaven (hell?) and earth. A fish swims through the ocean of water as a bird "swims" through the ocean of air. Fishes inhabit the dark depths, hidden from the eye of man, but at times come close to the land or are caught in nets and thus are revealed and sacrificed to and by man. The second attribute is the extraordinary number of eggs fishes produce— tens of thousands or millions—which makes them symbols of fecundity.

The cod, of course was unknown in the biblical lands, but it became most important in Europe as "denial" food during the Christian holy season of Lent. Over the centuries, elaborate rules and instructions were formulated for the preparation of the sacrificial meals. The rules were quite specific in the homes of the nobility. A fifteenth-century Northumberland "Household Book" states: "Such Braikfast is allowed daily in my Lordis house Every Lent to be bread, butter, a Quart of Bere, a Pece of salt fisch." The "salt fisch" in this case was salted dried cod.

Other salted fishes also figured in the diet of Europe in the Middle Ages. One of them was herring and it was almost as important as salt cod, but it had one chief drawback: its oily flesh did not keep as well as the nonoily flesh of the cod. And so the good housewife first used up the herring that would not last through the winter and saved the cod for the holy penance days of Lent in the spring. She followed the advice of people like Thomas Tusser, the British man of letters (1524–80) who wrote, "Spend herring first, save salt fish last: for salt fish is good when Lent is past." Not everyone liked cod, however. Many believed that eating it was a health hazard. They blamed it for causing a number of diseases—diseases probably caused by vitamin deficiencies rather than the salt fish itself.

The Protestant Reformation and the religious changes it instituted did not completely upset the requirements of the Lenten fast days, so salt cod maintained its important position on the market and in the home. To a large extent Lent determined the annual rhythm of commercial production of the salted fish and even the dates of sailing of vessels carrying the fish to Catholic countries on the Continent.

The Lenten obligation to fast was changed in modern times, however, and there were fears that the change would affect the entire fishing industry. Dr. Frederick W. Bell, Chief of the Branch of Economic Research of the Bureau of Commercial Fisheries, says that some fishery experts believed "this obligatory abstinence from meat has helped maintain the U.S. commercial fishing industry." But in 1966 Pope Paul VI issued an apostolic decree, *Poenitemini*, which relaxed the rules on fasting and abstinence during Lent and encouraged voluntary acts of penance. He ruled that Catholics need no longer fast and abstain from meat during Lenten weekdays, except on Fridays and Ash Wednesday. As part of his decree, the Pope delegated power to the Bishops of the Church to decide for their own countries whether to continue the rule of Friday abstinence, and those in the United States terminated obligatory meatless Fridays except during Lent.

The decree, however, had only slight effect on the American fishing industry, and even less effect in Europe. The New England Marine Resources Information Program reported in 1969 that there was no real upset to the U.S. fisheries as a result of the Pope's decree: "Although demand and landing prices for fish slipped sharply in the first nine months following the papal decree, they last year regained all the lost ground and prices reached new heights."

Though once important as a Lenten penance, the cod was so common that there was little mysticism attached to it. Instead of becoming an object of veneration, it became a figure of the vulgar. The dried cod, or stockfish, was a shapeless, colorless thing—a sorry-looking object that undoubtedly smelled strongly more often than not. To be a cod was to be laughed at and derided, to be a stupid lout. Falstaff, heaping abuse on young Prince Hal in *Henry IV, Part I*, begins, "You starvling, you elf-skin, you dried neat's tongue," building up to that ultimate insult, "you stockfish, O for breath to utter what is like thee!"

Nine old-time words—most of them nouns—use "cod" in a derisive manner. A cod was a practical joke, a bit of monkeyshine. It was a deception, a cheat, a fraud, a dirty gyp. A cod was a term of disparagement (a dumb cluck), a peculiar or eccentric person (a queer old duck), or simply an old fellow (a codger), a stupid person (a cod's head equals a dumbhead). "Cod" was also used as a verb: to cod one was to take him for a fool or deceive him; to hoax a simpleton by a falsehood (to spoof); or to engage in some light banter (to "cod around" was to give a razzing).

Two words that the fish did not contribute to the English language are "cod-end" and "cod-piece," although it seems as if it should have. The cod-end is the terminal part of a trawl or similar type of fishing net where the fish are accumulated while the trawl is dragged. Fishermen frequently call this part of the net the "bag," and this is another meaning of the word cod. This is also the derivation of the word "cod-piece," the appendage on the front of the tight-fitting trousers worn by men in the fifteenth and sixteenth centuries, which were sometimes padded to emphasize their masculinity.

The word cod in the sense of a bag is an Anglo-Saxon word (from before 1000 A.D. to about 1150 A.D.). It also meant a pod or shell (for peas and beans) and the scrotum. "Cod" meaning the fish *Gadus morhua* is a Middle-English word. Its origin is unknown but some language specialists suggest that it is from the Anglo-Saxon and refers to the supposed baglike shape of the fish.

American writers of the early nineteenth century were fond of using cod as a simile. Dion Boucicault, in a novel published in 1859, has one character tell another, "He's as deaf as a codfish." James Fenimore Cooper, author of the *Leatherstocking Tales*, writing in "The Pilot; a Tale of the Sea," concludes an argument between two characters by having one of them shout, "You are as dumb as a cod-fish!" A character in an 1856 novel, *The Three Brides, Love in a Cottage and Other Tales*, by Francis A. Durivage, promises, "I'll be mute as the codfish in the House of Representatives."

The cod that Durivage's character refers to can be seen today in the Massachusetts House of Representatives in Boston. The history of this particular cod began on March 17, 1784, when John Rowe rose from his seat in the House of Representatives and moved that "leave might be given to hang up the representation of a Cod Fish in the room where the House sit, as a memorial of the importance of the Cod-Fishery to the welfare of the Commonwealth, as had been usual formerly."

It is believed that Mr. Rowe's last reference was to another cod which apparently went up in smoke when the old State House (Town House) in Boston burned on December 9, 1747. The motion was seconded and passed, and a figure of a cod, approximately four feet, eleven inches long, was carved from a chunk of New England white pine and hung from the ceiling of the chamber. It remained there for more than a century, with a few minor excursions; it was taken down to be refurbished at least twice (although local historians quarrel over the exact number of times) and was stolen once as a prank by Harvard students.

In 1895, a new chamber was constructed in a wing of the State House and a debate ensued as to whether or not the "Sacred Cod" was also to be moved to the new quarters. As with many legislative bodies, a committee had to be formed before a decision could be made. The committee was to "prepare and report to the House the complete history of the codfish suspended in the chamber of the House of Representatives." The committee, comprised of Mr. Ernest W. Roberts of Chelsea, Mr. Richard W. Irwin of Northampton, and Mr. James A. Gallivan of Boston, reported back after two months' research as follows: "To those familiar with the history and development of Massachusetts there is nothing about the State House more interesting or suggestive than this codfish. It tells of commerce, war, diplomacy; of victories won by Massachusetts. It symbolizes the sources of our original wealth; the nursery of those mariners who manned the gun-decks of our frigates; our issues and struggles with England."

The Sacred Cod's place in history—as well as in the House chamber—was assured. Another committee of fifteen was formed to escort the carved effigy to its new place. The procedure was described by a contemporary writer:

> The committee immediately proceeded under the escort of Sergeant-at-Arms J. G. B. Adams to the discharge of its duty. Upon arriving at the chamber of the old House of Representatives, the emblem was lowered from its abiding place by John Kinnear, assistant doorkeeper of the house, wrapped in the American flag, deposited upon a bier, and borne to the House of Representatives. As the procession entered the House, the members arose, the historic emblem was received with a vigorous round of applause, and was deposited upon a table in front of the Speaker's desk.

The cod was repainted and suspended opposite the Speaker's chair, "between the two sets of central columns, and under the names 'Motley' and 'Parkman.' " It is still there today.

The importance of codfish to early America was recognized by the colonists long before the first wooden cod was hung in the Massachusetts House of Representatives. They used emblematic cods on seals, stamps, and letterheads. In 1661, a cod appeared on the corporate seal of the Plymouth Land Company. A cod emblem was used in 1686 by the Court of Quarter Sessions of the Peace and the Interior Court of Common Pleas of the Massachusetts Colony, and by the Middle Circuit Court of Common Pleas for the counties of Essex, Middlesex, and

Suffolk. The courts that condemned the Salem witches in 1692 included a cod on the official seals of the trial proceedings. The front page of the *Salem Gazette* in 1768 featured a coat of arms which consisted of a shield held by two Indians over a dove and an olive branch, with a codfish above all.

At least one of the hated British tax stamps of colonial America included a cod in its design. A two-penny tax stamp issued in 1755 depicted a cod with the motto, "Staple of the Massachusetts." And a cod was included on Colonial coins struck in 1776 and 1778.

Replicas of the cod were put to practical use by some early New Englanders who fashioned them into wind vanes. One of these was a wooden codfish studded with large copper nails that Paul Revere set on the roof of his shop in Canton, Massachusetts. The vanes, turning into the breeze like a fish turning into an ocean current, indicated changes in wind direction. With no other weather instruments available, the wind vane—showing these changes—gave a clue to the weather for the next day or two.

One of the oldest heraldic emblems depicting a cod is that of the Hanseatic league of northern Europe, a group of merchants from northern Germanic towns that took control of the herring fishery in the Baltic at the beginning of the fourteenth century. Later the league expanded its interests to include the cod fisheries, and established headquarters in Bergen, Norway. The coat of arms of the Hansa consists of half the German eagle in black against a yellow-gold field on the left side and a white stockfish (dried cod) with gold fins topped with a gold crown against a red field on the right side. This coat of arms may be seen in the Hanseatic Museum in Bergen.

The cod is mentioned in very few proverbs but it has inspired a small deluge of poems. One of the few proverbs is from Spain, and it has several versions. It states, in a rather ominous tone, *El bacalao muere por la boca.* This relates the simple truth that "the cod dies by its mouth," an obvious reference to fishing.

The poems are mostly in a light, humorous vein and were probably written as a reaction to the toil and drudgery of fishing. What is perhaps the funniest of the doggerel inspired by the cod doesn't even mention the fish—Arthur Scammel's "The Squid Jiggin' Ground" describes a scene in a Newfoundland harbor some time in the late nineteenth or early twentieth century, when the men of the village are trying to catch a supply of bait to use in the forthcoming cod fishing season. The poem is set to a folk tune and has become the unofficial national anthem of Newfoundland.

> This is the place where the fishermen gather,
> In oilskins and boots and Cape Anns battened down.
> All sizes of figgers with squid lines and jiggers.
> They congregate here on the Squid Jiggin' Ground.
> Some are workin' their jiggers while others are yarnin'.
> There's some standin' up and there's more lyin' down,
> While all kinds of fun, jokes, and tricks are begun
> As they wait for the squid on the Squid Jiggin' Ground.

The poem goes on to describe the men such as Uncle Bob Hawkins, who "wears six pairs of stockings," and old Uncle Billie, whose "whiskers are splattered wi' spots of the squid juice that's flyin' around." It concludes with the declaration that squid jigging is serious man's work, and that no dudes need apply.

A curious combination of Jonathan Swift's political fantasy, *Gulliver's Travels*, and the eighteenth-century English cod fishery off Newfoundland was set down in a poem written in 1727 by Alexander Pope. Glumdalclitch, a giantess of Brobdingnag, weeps because Gulliver has left. Pope abhors the waste of the copious salty flow of her anguish and pleads:

> O squander not thy grief; those tears command
> To weep upon our cod in Newfoundland.
> The plenteous pickle shall preserve the fish,
> And Europe taste thy sorrows in a dish.

An anonymous four-line poem written in the eighteenth century exhorts the creatures of the ocean depths to arouse themselves and celebrate:

> Ye finny monsters of the deep,
> Lift up your heads and shout!
> Ye cod fish from your hollows creep
> And wag your tails about!

This suggests a sort of witches' sabbath and reflects the general feeling prevalent until recently that the depths of the sea were inhabited

[15]

by all sorts of monstrous creatures. The occasional giant skate or grotesque goosefish that were caught with the familiar (but nonetheless ugly) cod gave credence to the beliefs about the existence of "finny monsters of the deep." We can almost imagine the doryman's logic: if such horrible creatures come so easily to man's view, what unseen monsters must there be in the ocean deeps?

One of the lighter rhymes about the cod couples biology and behavior:

> The codfish lays a million eggs,
>   The homely hen lays one.
> But the codfish never cackles
>   To tell you what she's done.
> And so we scorn the codfish,
>   While the humble hen we prize.
> Which only goes to show that
>   It pays to advertise.

The New Englander's fondness for a codfish chowder or a steaming serving of "Cape Cod turkey" (dried salt cod prepared in a sauce) is expressed in another little four-liner. We can imagine a Bostonian far from home writing that he misses a good codfish dinner. The recipient of the letter obliges in a way that must have presented the post office with a massive problem.

> He pasted down a sheet of postage stamps
>   From the snout clear down to the tail,
> Put on a special delivery stamp, and
>   Sent the cod by mail.

It is not surprising to find the cod included in the vast repertoire of sailor's chanties, since it was a common food on the old sailing ships. Chanties were sung as an accompaniment to work on the ship that required team effort, such as walking the capstan to lift the anchor or hauling a line to raise a sail.

Some of the chanties had more than one version:

> Gloucester girls they have no combs,
>   Heave away, heave away!
> They comb their hair with codfish bones,

We're bound for South Australia.
Heave away, my bully bully boys, heave away, heave away.
Heave away, why don't you make a noise?
We're bound for South Australia.
Gloucester boys they have no sleds,
They slide down hill on codfish heads.
Heave away, my bully bully boys, heave away, heave away.

The other version of the chanty switches the locale to Cape Cod and adds a bit of nonsensical information about the tabbies of that sandy, windswept spit:

Cape Cod girls they have no combs.
They comb their hair with codfish bones.
Cape Cod boys they have no sleds,
They slide down dunes on codfish heads.
Cape Cod cats they have no tails.
They lost them all in sou'east gales.

One further kind of rhyme—also anonymous and old—is a brain-teaser that makes a play on the letters in the word cod. It is simply titled "Enigma on Cod."

Cut off my head and singular I act.
Cut off my tail, and plural I appear.
Cut off my head and tail and, wondrous fact,
Although my middle's left, there's nothing there.
What is my head cut off? A sounding sea.
What is my tail cut off? A flowing river,
In whose translucent depths I fearless play,
Parent of sweetest sounds, yet mute forever.

The cod also appears in folk literature. One fairy tale concerns a fisherman who catches a fish that is really a special personage (either a changeling royal human or a sort of king-of-all-fishes). The fish pleads for its life and promises the fisherman one wish if he will let it go. In Southeast Asia the fish is an eel; in France it is a perch; in Germany it is a flounder; in a Scandinavian version the fish is a cod.

The fisherman releases the talking cod and rushes home to tell his wife of their good fortune. She immediately wishes for a finer cottage.

[17]

The wish is granted but the wife, a greedy, grasping shrew, is not satisfied and demands that her husband force the cod to bestow another wish on them. He returns to the sea and calls out,

> Codfish, codfish in the sea,
> Come, I pray, and talk to me.
> My wife at home, Dame Isabel,
> Sent me here, a tale to tell.

The codfish grants the second wish, to replace the cottage with a castle, but again the wife is not satisfied. In turn she demands, and is granted, wishes to become a queen in a palace, and then the Pope. Still not satisfied, she finally demands to become equal to The Creator. The fisherman returns tremblingly to the sea and in a frightened voice, calls out,

> Codfish, codfish in the sea,
> Come, I pray, and talk to me.
> My wife at home, Dame Isabel,
> Wishes what I fear to tell.

The poor fisherman [stood] in terror, for a dreadful storm had arisen and he could scarcely stand on his feet. Ships were wrecked, boats tossed to and fro, and rocks rolled into the sea.

In his terror and confusion he heard a voice from amid the storm:

"Your wife wishes to be equal to the Creator. Go home, man, and find her again in the dirty hovel by the sea!"

He went home, to find the glories, the riches, and the palaces vanished, and his wife sitting in the old hut, an example of the consequences of impious ambition. (From a Danish adaptation of *Grimm's Fairy Tales*.)

The cod has found its way into the food tradition of many parts of the world not only as a Lenten fasting food but also for other holiday seasons and times of celebration.

In Sweden and Norway, the culinary highpoint of Christmas is the preparation and eating of *lutefisk*, usually made from unsalted, air-dried cod, or stockfish. To make the traditional dish, the stockfish is soaked in fresh water for four or five days and then soaked in a lye solution for one day. After this treatment the fish has a bland flavor and a texture somewhat like boiled eggwhite. It is served with melted butter or a white sauce.

The *lutefisk* tradition is said to be a carryover from pre-Reformation times, when all big holidays and celebrations were preceded by a period of fasting. When food supplies were short after the winter, the only dish one could be sure of having for the table was dried cod. *Lutefisk* was, therefore, not only a Christmas treat, but was also enjoyed at Eastertime.

In Denmark, a traditional New Year's Eve dinner includes boiled cod and potatoes, served with either mustard sauce or drawn butter.

In Massachusetts, a "good dish of codfish" is one of the nine traditional items served at the Forefathers' Feast celebrated each year on December 22 (New Calendar), commemorating the landing of the Pilgrims on December 11, 1620 (Old Calendar). The first celebration of the Forefathers' Feast took place in Plymouth on December 22, 1769. The menu for this first memorial banquet included:

> One large baked Indian whortleberry pudding.
> One dish of *sauquetach*,
> One dish of clams,
> One dish of oysters,
> One dish of eels,
> One good dish of codfish,
> A haunch of venison,
> A big apple pie, and
> A round of cranberry tarts with cheese.

Whortleberries are better known now as huckleberries, and the Indian dish *sauquetach* is that familiar mixture of beans and corn, succotash.

The special place that the cod occupies in the hearts of New Englanders is well illustrated by the story of a young street urchin who tapped on the back door of an old Boston lady. He had been fishing down at the harbor. Would she like to buy some nice fresh cod for her supper? "How much?" asked the lady. "Ten cents each," was the reply. The lady was of the school that held the cod sacred. "Little boy," she scolded, "never, never sell cod for less than twenty-five cents!"

Cod on bottom on Grand Banks. Depth: 1,350 feet. (National Marine Fisheries Service)

3

Natural History of the Cod

A FISHERY BIOLOGIST once calculated how many cod there would be in the world if all the eggs spawned by all female cod in *one* spawning season were to hatch and survive to adulthood: the number was astronomical. He concluded that the oceans of the world, from shore to shore and from bottom to surface, would be one mass of wriggling cod, with no room for anything else.

The basis for the skyrocketing numbers in the biologist's calculations is the enormous fecundity of the cod. The number of eggs any species of fish will spawn varies with the species and the size of the individual. Trout, for example, may spawn only a few hundred eggs, while others, like the sea herring, may spawn 30,000 or so. But the cod spawns eggs by the millions.

Probably no one has actually counted all the eggs in a female cod, but by a painstaking method of sampling and weighing, biologists have accurately estimated the number. A very large cod may contain as many as 9 million eggs. Such a champion fish would weigh about seventy-five pounds and measure sixty inches long. Cod weighing between thirty and forty pounds (about thirty-five to forty-five inches long) may produce 3 to 4 million eggs each year. For the general run of cod (ten to twenty-five pounds and thirty to forty inches long), the average production of one female is probably slightly more than a million eggs annually.

No one has seen the spawning of wild schools of cod, since it takes place in the depths of the open ocean. But biologists have observed spawning cod in large saltwater ponds in hatcheries, and their notes give us a good idea what the spawning act in the depths of the sea must be like.

G. M. Dannevig, a Danish biologist, reported in 1887 that "a sort of pairing between spawning cod" took place, with the males swimming belly up under the females. The genital apertures of the pair were turned toward each other, and the sperm emitted by the male floated upward to fertilize the eggs spawned by the female. Dannevig saw some males that seemed to hold the females by laying their pectoral fins (which are in the same relative position on the cod's body as our arms are on ours) against the females' sides. These observations are apparently the first recorded despite the fact that the cod had been an object of careful scrutiny—economic as well as scientific—for well over 500 years.

Some additional details of the spawning act were supplied in 1892 by Adolph Nielsen, a Norwegian biologist employed by Newfoundland as Superintendent of Fisheries. The cod hatchery at Trinity Bay, Newfoundland, had a spawning pond forty-eight feet long, twenty-three feet wide, and eleven feet deep. Here Nielsen watched spawning cod, and his notes corroborate Dannevig's observations. "It is remarkable," he said, "to notice how exactly they are able to keep their vents in the one and right position during this act, although they are swimming swiftly and often turn right around from one direction to another very rapidly." The vigorous swimming undoubtedly serves a useful purpose in insuring the maximum fertilization of ova.

A third observation of a "sort of pairing" during the spawning of the cod was made by the Norwegian fishery scientist Gunnar Rollefsen at the Biological Station at Trondheim in the spring of 1934. He noticed that the eggs and sperm were whirled together by the vigorous movement of the fish's broad tail fins.

The males of some fishes go through elaborate courtship rituals of nuzzling, biting, nudging, displays or posturing with fins held erect, and, in certain tropical fishes, dazzling color changes. These rituals, according to fish behaviorists, excite the female and help to prepare her for the spawning act. It is not known for certain if the cod exhibits any courtship behavior, but there is a suggestion of such behavior in some of the movements Rollefsen saw. He wrote: "As a first step the male was swimming with his head resting on the crown of the female, gradually he sank sideways, and finally male and female were swimming belly against belly."

The factors that trigger the spawning impulse in the male cod are largely a mystery. It may possibly be length of day, as it is with birds. In the spawning season, the usual cod habitat—300 feet or more below the surface of the sea, where sunlight penetrates but little—is a world of perpetual twilight or dark, even during the brightest part of the surface day. But dim though it may be, the light does vary with the seasons, and this may be enough to stimulate spawning.

It is possible, too, that changes in the temperature of the water exert some influence on spawning cod. During the late winter and early spring months, when the cod spawns, the water is about as cold as it ever gets during the yearly cycle. The temperature varies somewhat from place to place, and it may range from 32 to 45 degrees Fahrenheit. During the warmest part of the year, in early autumn, the water is only slightly warmer—38 to 53 degrees Fahrenheit. Cod are amazingly sensitive to changes in water temperature of only .05 degree. Perhaps it is the decline in water temperature and the subsequent period of cold that trigger the spawning urge.

In this gloomy and cold environment the cod performs its "sort of pairing," to liberate the great masses of eggs and clouds of sperm for the perpetuation of its kind. The eggs that have swelled the female's belly are released and are swirled about with the milky clouds of sperm during the vigorous spawning act. It appears that the eggs are released in batches over a period of hours or days. This is borne out by the observations made of a female in an aquarium tank in Cullercoats (England). She spawned six times in seventeen days, at intervals of three to four days.

From the moment of spawning, the codfish eggs are subjected to forces and events that prevent an ocean of wriggling codfish from becoming reality. Of the several million eggs each female spawns, only about one egg of each million succeeds in completing the full cycle of growth to become a mature cod. The greatest initial loss is of eggs that are not fertilized. Despite the gyrations of the spawning pair, many of the eggs do not contact sperm, and they sink to the ocean floor and die.

The eggs that are fertilized absorb a minute amount of seawater, swell, become buoyant, and begin a slow journey upward to the surface. Many of the earliest observations on cod eggs and their development were made by the Norwegian biologist G. O. Sars. In 1864 and for a number of years afterward, he reported on the prosperous cod fisheries in the Lofoten Islands of Norway. His studies were eye-openers for Sars in at least one aspect. For years he had shared the common idea that cod eggs, like those of the herring and other fishes, settled to the bottom for their development. Fishermen (who are keen observers of natural history) told him that at certain seasons the eggs of the codfish could be seen floating in such quantities "as to make the water appear quite thick." Sars soon found this was no exaggeration and wrote that "with a large gauze net I could have taken tons of it."

It is not known for certain how fast cod eggs rise to the surface, but David Miller, in Woods Hole, found that the very similar haddock eggs rose at the rate of three and a half feet per hour. Thus a cod egg fertilized at or near the ocean floor, at about fifty fathoms, and rising at the same rate as haddock eggs would take about thirty hours to reach the surface.

During the slow ascent to the surface many eggs fail to develop properly and die. Robert R. Marak of Woods Hole found a large concentration of dead and dying cod eggs just south of Nova Scotia. The abnormal eggs covered an area of at least a thousand square miles, with approximately a million eggs per square mile. Microscopic examination of the eggs showed that the embryos were defective and had stopped developing, and perhaps (it was suggested) the eggs had been prematurely spawned.

The fertilized eggs that reach the surface become part of the surface plankton, the drifting plants and animals of the sea. Sir Alister Hardy, the eminent British planktologist, describes how "their little transparent spheres drift with the moving waters and develop into the young fry." The floating eggs are at the mercy of the elements. Experiments have shown that mechanical agitation damages cod eggs, and Rollefsen postulated that agitation from storms at sea may kill them. Sudden extremes of cold or heat also may kill cod eggs.

The rising, and later drifting, eggs also face the immense hazards of predatory animals of the sea. The hostile environment abounds with schools of swiftly moving herring that devour untold millions of the eggs. Drifting crablike creatures prey on the floating, helpless eggs. And in the realm of microscopic life, cod eggs fall prey to marine bacteria and fungi.

Despite the great size of most spawning cod, the eggs themselves are tiny. The eggs vary from one thirty-second to three-thirty-seconds of an inch in diameter; seventeen of them placed in a row would measure only one inch. The eggs spawned in cold waters tend to be larger than those spawned in warm waters because of the increased yolk that must nourish the embryo cod during the longer period of development that is the rule in cold water. It takes about ten days for the eggs to hatch in water of 47 degrees, but it takes forty days or more in water of 32 degrees.

As part of his research in the Lofoten Islands, Sars collected cod eggs and watched them develop into larval codfish. Later, he suggested establishing hatcheries to collect, fertilize, and cultivate cod eggs and thus carry them through the first few critical weeks away from the hazards of the open sea. Cod hatcheries subsequently became an important part of European and American fish conservation programs—but an unsuccessful part, as will be discussed in the final chapter.

The newly hatched cod, called larvae, are about three-sixteenths of an inch long. At first they depend for food on the pendulous yolk sac attached to their abdomen but by the sixth day after hatching the yolk is absorbed and the larvae must begin to forage for living food. Although it is now only about a quarter of an inch long, the young cod becomes an active predator—hunter as well as hunted. The future existence of the little fish depends as much on finding a plentiful supply of food as on escaping the enemies that surround it.

The food of the young cod is minute plankton animals, including the larvae of barnacles, lobsters, shrimps, and crabs, and little worms. Frequently the pursuer becomes too eager and tries to eat animals it can not swallow. Robert Marak observed in the laboratory that the larval cod often took food animals into its mouth that were much too large to be swallowed.

When the young cod are only about one month old and perhaps three-quarters of an inch long, many of them form a rather curious relationship with the red jellyfish, *Cyanea*. The floating bell of this sea animal may be several inches to a foot or more in diameter, and from it hang the long, deadly tentacles that can sting and even kill the small sea creatures the jellyfish depends on for food. Although not as dangerous as the Portuguese man-of-war, the specialized stinging cells in the tentacles of *Cyanea* are capable of producing painful welts on the unlucky human bather that touches it. How then is the tiny cod able to live and swim among the *Cyanea*'s numerous stinging threads?

[25]

Sars thought that perhaps the jellyfish exerted some "magic power" over the fish to keep them under the bell, but after careful study he found that theirs was a mutually beneficial arrangement. The jelly-fishes, he noticed, were infested with a parasitic crustacean, *Hyperia*, that ate its way deep into the host's bell. But, he reported, "I invariably found some of these crustaceans in the stomachs of the young codfish." It seemed clear to him then that the cod lived with apparent immunity among the tentacles, ridding the *Cyanea* of its parasites and feeding on scraps and tiny organisms captured by the jellyfish for its own food. The tentacles also afforded the cod a place of refuge from its enemies. But life under the jellyfish is not quite a codfish utopia. Occasionally they swim too close to the bell, become entangled in the deadly threads, and are killed. The *Cyanea* then loses no time in making a meal of its former partner.

Two months after beginning life as millions of tiny eggs floating in the cold North Atlantic, the survivors have grown to between one inch and one and a quarter inch long. The larvae do not look like their parents; their fins are not yet formed, their bodies are long and slender, and their grotesque, overly large heads are dominated by a pair of large, very dark eyes. But at this point the fry begins to look more like a small cod.

Now the cod begin what is probably the most strenuous and most dangerous migration they ever undertake—the trip to the bottom. Adult cod are bottom fish. Although they occasionally come to the surface, especially when they are in eager pursuit of capelin or herring, they usually swim near or sometimes even touch the ocean floor. They can live in water as deep as 1,500 feet or as shallow as eighteen to thirty feet deep, but they are found most often in depths of from 120 to 900 feet. The young cod, which have up to now been nearly help-less drifters in the surface waters, swim to the bottom where they will spend the rest of their lives. Most of the fish are in shallow, near-shore waters but some are off-shore in deep water. It is not known for certain how long it takes to make the descent into the uniformly cold and dark depths of the sea, but it probably is a matter of two weeks or so. The fish must acclimate to the increasing pressure as they move down-ward.

Michael Graham, the British fishery expert, suggests that the descent to the bottom is the most critical part of the cod's life because the young fish is subjected to increasing pressure that has unknown effects.

[26]

The relatively warm surface waters change to the increasing cold of the mid-depths. Food is scarcer in the mid-depths, too, and when the small cod finally reach the ocean floor they must learn to prey on an entirely different world of potential food creatures. Crabs, pelecypods (bivalve shellfish), gastropods (snails), small shrimps, and various worms are available instead of the smaller floating creatures in the surface waters. Graham believes that many of the cod become weakened from lack of food while they are learning to change their feeding habits and fall prey to pollock, spiny dogfish, and other predatory fishes. The young cod find no refuge among their own kind, either, because the adults are cannibals who would just as soon make a meal of their progeny as any other small fishes. Even cod that have grown to seven or eight inches long may be greedily snatched up by the adults.

Once they are firmly established in the community of groundfishes, however, the cod feed on a varied diet. Shellfish of all kinds form a large part of their food, and cod stomachs are mines of information for students of mollusks. Years ago, before naturalists had the many specialized deep-sea dredges they now use for collecting shell specimens, the stomach contents of cod in the market stalls were favorite exploring grounds for rare shells. For example, the first known specimen of the giant deep-sea scallop (*Placopecten magellanicus*) was reported in 1845 from a shell found in a cod caught off the coast of Maine. The interest of naturalists was aroused by this discovery, and dredging for more specimens of this shellfish disclosed grounds where the bottom was paved with the almost-dinner-plate-size scallops. A little experimental tasting by an unknown pioneer showed that the meaty muscle or "eye" of the meat portion of the scallop was a seafood delicacy when fried or stewed. It was not long before a full-fledged scallop fishery developed off the New England and Middle Atlantic states. Today, the industry lands about 7.4 million pounds of scallop meats annually (representing perhaps 110 million individual scallops), most of it at the port of New Bedford, Massachusetts.

The cod swallows shellfish whole and its powerful stomach juices digest out the soft meats. The big shells (up to seven inches long) of the large sea clam *Spisula* are often found neatly stacked, six and seven deep like dessert dishes, in cod stomachs. When the indigestible shells finally are expelled, they help form shell middens. Cod also feed on large moonsnails (*Polynices*), crabs, lobsters, brittle stars, and several kinds of shrimp.

Many kinds of fish are eaten. Cod particularly go after the schooling fishes—herring, menhaden, alewives—and in the northern part of their range, around Newfoundland, for example, cod voraciously chase capelin (*Mallotus*). They also pursue and gorge on squid at every chance, a fact that was quickly put to good use by the handline and longline fishermen off the rugged Newfoundland coast, who learned that squid made "the finest kind o' bait." But in order to catch the cod, the fishermen first have to catch the bait. This they do by "jigging" for squid with a multihooked artificial lure. The squid, thinking the lure is some helpless prey, grab the jig and are caught. There is almost a carnival atmosphere when a school of squid is sighted in a bay or cove, and the men of the fishing hamlet go out in their dories—"all kinds of figgers with squid lines and jiggers"—to catch the bait.

While the variety of marine organisms in the cod diet are interesting enough, it is the nonfood items found among the stomach contents that have made the cod almost legendary. Such indigestible items as pieces of wood and scraps of clothing, old boots, oil cans, a rubber doll, a cigarette case, and other odds and ends have been found from time to time in cod stomachs, probably dropped from fishing boats, freighters, and passenger ships. (One of the principal shipping lanes between Europe and North America passes over the rich cod fishing grounds of the Grand Banks.) Experiments reported in the *Journal of the Marine Biological Association* (United Kingdom) on cod in captivity, and the numerous observations of fishermen, suggest that cod capture moving objects by sight, and since they can see clearly for only a few feet, they probably mistake the boots and other objects for fish or other edible prey as the items sink through the water.

One codfish dressed aboard a trawler had a part of a set of false teeth in its stomach. With a little judicious guessing we can piece together the probable circumstances that led to the fish ingesting the dentures. A seasick passenger on a passing vessel leaned over the rail in a moment of extreme nausea and, not having time to remove his bridgework, lost the false teeth along with his dinner. As the white teeth flashed through the murky depths, a hungry cod snapped at them and swallowed them, perhaps mistaking them for a silvery herring.

A strange and somewhat eerie item retrieved from a cod's stomach was a woman's wedding ring, and the circumstances that led up to the find caused some confusion and consternation about the feeding habits of codfish. The situation may also have caused some less hardy souls to forgo codfish dinners for a while—or forever. In 1871, a St. John's, Newfoundland, fisherman was dressing a large codfish in preparation for salting it. As the stomach contents spilled out onto the deck he noticed a glittering object among the shells, fish bones, and crab remains. The object was a gold wedding ring, brightly polished from the bath of stomach juices and the churning of digestion. Initials and a date, however, could still be read inside the band. The local newspaper heard about it and initiated some detective work to track down the former owner of the ring. The owner, they discovered, had been a passenger aboard the steamship *Anglo Saxon* and was lost at sea when the vessel was wrecked off Chance Cove, Newfoundland. Did the cod pick the dead woman's bones? Probably not. The ship had foundered ten years before the ring was found and the drowned passengers' remains would have long been scattered by the ocean currents. It is fairly safe (if less exciting) to assume that the cod had picked up the ring from the bottom.

There is a happy sequel to the story. The dead woman's surviving son was contacted and happily received the memento of his mother. In gratitude he paid the fisherman a reward of £50.

Frequently, stones also are found in the stomachs of cod. Old-time cod fishermen, who had to be expert seafarers to wrest a living from the sea, believed that their quarry was likewise an expert seafarer. The schools of cod, they knew, moved widely from place to place on the banks. Consequently, the fishermen reasoned that the cod had swallowed stones for ballast in preparation for a long journey, the same way that a ship is loaded with ballast to make it sit properly in the water. Another explanation offered was that the cod had foreknowledge of severe storms at sea and so swallowed the stones to help it maintain a position near the ocean bottom, away from the influence of the storm waves.

Neither interesting tale is true. We know now that the stones are swallowed for the anemones, hydroids, and other animals growing on them. Once the stomach juices digest the animals, the stones are passed through the digestive tract with the shells, crab remains, and other indigestibles.

The diet of fishes and squids (and not of such curiosities as false teeth and wedding rings) enable the cod to grow at a rapid rate. During the first year of its life, a cod attains a size of about six or seven inches. This varies considerably; in the relatively warm waters off

Nantucket, a fish may grow to eight inches during the first year, whereas in the colder waters of the North Sea it may grow only to five inches.

By the end of the second year, Nantucket cod have usually doubled their first year's size and average about fourteen inches long. The end of the third year sees a tripling of the first year's growth, with the cod now averaging about twenty-two inches. In European waters the lengths for the second and third years are eight inches and twelve inches.

The great variation in the rate of growth from place to place over the range inhabited by the fish is influenced by water temperature, availability and quality of food, the genetic background of the individual fish and the population, and probably by factors of which we have no knowledge as yet.

The geographic variations in cod growth rates are striking. The fastest growing cod are those of the Irish Sea. In six years, they grow to a length of thirty-seven inches. In the same length of time, the slowest-growing cod from off the coast of Sweden grow to a length of only sixteen inches. The famed cod of the Grand Banks off Newfoundland have an intermediate growth rate, and reach a length of twenty-four inches over the span of six years; they are nearly twelve years old before they reach a size equivalent to the six-year-old Irish Sea cod.

The rate of growth of most cod begins to slow when they are about three years old. At this age they become sexually mature and, a large part of the energy from the food they eat is diverted to the production and development of eggs and sperm.

Cod grow to very respectable sizes. In fact, some of them are among the biggest of all fishes. G. B. Goode mentions five large cod caught off the Massachusetts coast in the 1800's that ranged between 100 and 160 pounds. In 1838, a cod taken on Georges Bank weighed 136 pounds when dressed and it probably weighed 180 pounds alive. All these were caught by commercial fishermen, but even sportfishermen have landed some jumbos. In July 1873, Miss Fannie Belis of St. Louis, Missouri, was fishing from the yacht *United States* in the Atlantic Ocean off Gloucester, Massachusetts. Much to her delight, and no doubt the chagrin of her male companions, she caught and landed a cod that weighed in at 130 pounds. The official International Game Fish Association record, however, is a fish weighing ninety-eight pounds and twelve ounces caught by Alphonse Bielevich in June 1969.

This record-smasher measured five feet, three inches long and was taken from the waters off Newburyport, Massachusetts. The world-record cod for women anglers is a forty-eight-and-a-half-pound fish caught by Mrs. Estele Lindsay in January 1967. She was fishing aboard a party boat, *Viking*, out of Montauk, New York. Another big cod, but not quite a record—seventy-two pounds—was caught by fourteen-year-old Marty Pastore, also out of Montauk, in June 1969.

The giant among cod is one caught by a commercial fisherman with a linetrawl off the Massachusetts coast in May 1895. Often called the "Patriarch Cod," it weighed 211½ pounds and was over six feet long. It is doubtful if the seas will ever again produce such a codfish. The modern intensive commercial fisheries catch the cod before they can grow much larger than three feet long.

There is, unfortunately, no estimation of the age of the Patriarch Cod, but there is no doubt it was a very old fish. It may very well have achieved the maximum age of fifty years that C. C. Taylor, U.S. Bureau of Commercial Fisheries biologist, reported as theoretically possible for the species. Cod are known to have lived to thirteen years of age in captivity and to twenty-two years in nature, but it is likely that even older cod are present in the population.

Although biologists speak of determining the age of a fish, in actual practice they frequently can only estimate the age because of the techniques that are used. In most bony fishes (that is, fishes other than sharks, skates, rays, and other cartilaginous fishes), periodic markings something like the growth rings that can be counted on tree stumps are formed during the course of the year on the scales and on certain bones, including the otoliths, or ear bones. The scales of a cod, in fact, look something like the top of a tree stump but experience has shown that the scales are poor indicators of age for cod. The usual practice today is to "read" the ages from cod otoliths.

Otoliths—pearly-white calcium carbonate bodies that look something like narrow lima beans—form part of the balance mechanism in the cod's skull. They grow by adding on layers, but the chemical composition of the concentric shells varies slightly during different seasons of the year. As a result, when an otolith is broken or sawed crossways, the cut face or cross section reveals light and dark zones. Generally, the light zones are formed during the season of warmer water and the dark zones are formed during the season of colder water. The biologists examine the cross-sectioned otolith under the microscope and count the dark, or winter, zones on the assumption that one dark zone is formed each year.

As the cod grows older, the most recently formed zones are narrow and the outermost ones may be thin hairlines. It is possible to miss some of the thinnest zones and underestimate the age of the oldest fish. For that reason, the estimated age of twenty-two years, made by Paul M. Hansen, a Danish biologist, for a fish in the natural population could be a conservative estimate.

Variations in the growth rates of cod from different areas is one of the ways of identifying cod groups. Other ways include marking the fish with tags, studying the incidence of infestation of various parasites, and, more recently, studying cod blood groups (similar to human blood types of the A, B, and O series). By combining these techniques, biologists can speak of Grand Banks cod, Gulf of Maine cod, or Irish Sea cod in somewhat the same way as we speak of people as Englishmen, Frenchmen, or Americans.

Marking cod with tags is also used to determine the various migrations the fish may make during its lifetime. The kinds of tags used on cod are legion, but biologists have yet to design the perfect tag. In 1894, Dr. C. G. J. Petersen, a Danish biologist, devised a tag that consisted of two brightly colored discs, each about a half inch in diameter, attached with a pin or wire to the operculum (gill cover), back muscles, or other part of the cod. This tag was very successful and is still used today. One of the most recent experiments in marking cod with Petersen tags was done by John P. Wise. From 1955 to 1959, Wise tagged approximately 2,000 cod with the tag in the waters off New England; 14 per cent of the marked fish were returned by fishermen.

Not all tags work out well. Between 1897 and 1901, Hugh M. Smith, a pioneer fishery biologist with the former U.S. Bureau of Fisheries, tagged 4,000 cod with numbered ¾-by-¼-inch pieces of sheet copper attached to the fish with fine copper wire. Less than 4 per cent of the tagged fish were caught again, and most biologists believe that the wire worked its way through the flesh of the cod and dropped off.

Later, between 1901 and 1923, Bureau of Fisheries investigators tried metal tags of the kind clamped to the ears of cattle, attaching them to the thick part of the tail of the cod. The tags were made of several different kinds of metal, including silver, aluminum, copper, silver-plated copper, and monel. Biologists estimated that as many as 60 per cent of the fish had lost the tags within the first year.

Another tag often used on cod is the Lea tag, named for Einar Lea, the Norwegian biologist who developed it. The tag consists of a small waterproof plastic tube that contains a rolled-paper message of instructions to the finder. The tube usually is attached with a wire bridle to the dorsal muscles of the fish. Wise had used the Lea tag on some of the cod in his experiments. Frank D. McCracken, a Canadian fishery scientist, got a 30 per cent return on nearly 3,000 cod tagged with Lea tags.

One very successful mark for cod was a combination of two tags—the Lea tag and an internal tag. The latter was a small tab of plastic actually placed in the body cavity of the fish through a small incision made in the belly wall. The incision healed quickly after the tagged fish was released in the sea, usually leaving only a tiny scar. This was the chief fault of the internal tag—it was not always seen when the fish was caught again. A group of Woods Hole biologists connected the Lea tag to the internal tag with a short, fine chain. When the internal part was inserted in the fish, the Lea tag hung outside where it could easily be seen.

All of these efforts to develop better tags were made to learn how the cod lived, and especially how and where it migrated. The answers gained from tagging experiments have turned up some curious facts about cod journeys in the depths of the sea.

Some groups of cod are relatively stationary and may move only a few dozen miles during their lifetime. Other groups, and some individuals, may make extensive migrations. Two of the groups that make long migrations are the Bear Island cod, studied by British fishery scientist Geoffrey Trout, and the New Jersey coastal cod studied by William C. Schroeder and later by John Wise.

The Bear Island cod inhabit the cold Arctic waters between the northern tip of Norway and Spitzbergen and are fished heavily by distant-water trawlers from Great Britain, Denmark, Norway, and other nations. Most of the cod involved in the migrations studied by Trout were immature. In the summer, these cod move northward to the banks around Spitzbergen and feed in the productive waters. With the coming of winter, the fish move southward to Bear Island, and many move still farther south, some to the southeast Barents Sea, others to the Lofoten Islands (off the northwest coast of Norway) to spawn.

With information gleaned from catches of tagged fish, scientists can deduce what the fish are doing. Geoffrey Trout discovered that the

Bear Island cod do not feed during the winter spawning season but use food reserves stored as fat in the liver to maintain themselves and to produce eggs and sperm. By the time the cod have completed their spawning they are thin and weakened. Trout suggested that when the cod move northward to the feeding grounds they drift with little swimming effort in the northward-flowing West Spitzbergen Current. This river-in-the-sea carries the cod and allows them to conserve energy until they begin to feed again.

Trout deduced also that light probably was a factor in triggering the southward movement of the now-fattened cod and starting them on the journey to the spawning grounds. As the waning Arctic days bring shorter and shorter periods of light, the shoals of cod retreat before the reduced illumination and move south. During the summer, their usual haunts are on the banks in fifty to a hundred fathoms, but in the winter they seek the deeps, up to 200 fathoms, where they are presumed to be either actually touching the bottom or close enough to receive some stimuli from it. During the winter, little or no light reaches the ocean floor at these depths, and in the black of the abyss the cod become oriented to the water movement over the bottom. They either swim just enough to keep from being swept backward or they actively swim forward against the current and then drift back to maintain the same sort of relative position in the area.

The New Jersey coastal cod that Schroeder and Wise studied spawn along the Middle Atlantic coast, especially off New Jersey. In the spring, they migrate in great numbers northward to the waters off southern New England, particularly on Nantucket Shoals.

While light is probably one of the facts that triggers these great movements of cod, water temperature must also be important. Some of the migrating cod are thus in search of water temperatures that are comfortable. The body temperature of the cod, a cold-blooded creature, is determined by the temperature of the water it inhabits. If the temperature is too low or too high it grows sluggish and may die. For example, the rising springtime temperatures off the Middle Atlantic coast induce New Jersey coastal cod to seek the relatively cooler waters off New England. With the coming of autumn and a decrease in water temperatures off New England, the cod journey south toward the warmer waters. Although cod can live in temperatures from nearly as low as the freezing point of salt water (28 degrees Farenheit) to almost as high as 68 degrees Fahrenheit, they seem to prefer temperatures between 32 and 52 degrees Fahrenheit. Most of the large commercial catches of cod are made at the lower end of this temperature range, and the larger individuals are caught in the colder water. This fact of cod life was turned to the advantage of commercial fishermen as a result of research conducted by Canadian scientists. In a letter to fishermen, biologist R. A. McKenzie of the St. Andrews Biological Station advised them to carry thermometers aboard their vessels and periodically measure the temperature of the water. Armed with the knowledge of the preferred water temperatures, the fishermen could search out "cod water" and fish where the temperatures seemed right. The thermometers were used for a number of years but gradually discarded as oceanographers learned more about the temperature structure of the sea. The development of refined research instruments that could measure the temperature from the surface to the depths showed that at certain seasons of the year the surface water (measured by the fishermen's thermometers) could be as much as ten degrees or more warmer or colder than the deep water where the cod were.

The most compelling journey of the cod is the annual spawning migration made during the late winter and early spring, when the fish form dense schools on the spawning grounds. Here the males easily find the females to carry out their "sort of pairing." Commercial fishermen have learned to take advantage of the schooling of spawning cod to catch great quantities of them. In the famed fishery on the Grand Bank of Newfoundland modern trawlers from over a dozen nations often take thirty-five tons of cod each in two hours of fishing during the spring spawning concentration.

The usual journey performed by a cod is only a few hundred miles from the place of release to the place where it finally was caught again, but some cod make exceptional migrations. One tagged cod made a 2,500-mile trip. The time between tagging and recapture is sometimes as much as five years. Of course, we have no way of knowing where or how far the cod may have wandered during that time; it is like a man's biography that reports only the date and place of birth and the date and place of death with no details about the life between those events.

A curious sort of individual migration is made by very large cod that wander from their native waters like old rogues, never to return. Such one-way trips are made by cod in the waters off New England and the Canadian Maritimes. The fish swim to the northeast, urged on by some mysterious drive about which we have no knowledge at the present time.

One fact turned up by tagging studies is that cod can hardly be classed as greyhounds of the sea. The average speed is about three miles per day, but Wise reports one cod that journeyed at the rate of sixteen miles per day for nearly a month, in migrating from East Greenland to West Greenland. In the laboratory, the maximum swimming speed of cod has been measured as about four miles per hour.

In all of the tagging experiments yet reported, only a few cod have made a transatlantic journey from North American waters eastward to European waters, and until 1962 none had made the journey from east to west. In that year, two British fishery scientists, J. A. Gulland and G. R. Williamson, reported in the European scientific journal *Nature* that a cod tagged in the North Sea in June 1957 had been recaptured on January 1962 on the Grand Bank of Newfoundland.

4

The Varieties of Cod

TO THE GLOUCESTER DORYMAN, cod was, simply, *the fish*. And in Newfoundland, the courts ruled that "whenever the word 'fish' is unqualified it must be taken to mean Codfish." To the French, the Spanish, the Portuguese, the Italians, the Germans, the Norwegians, and the Russians cod is *morue, bacalao, bacalhau, baccala, kabaljau, torsk,* and *treska*. These names usually refer to *Gadus morhua*, the scientific name given the common cod by Linnaeus in 1758.

Over the years, it became evident to fishery scentists that there was not one cod but many. Some are merely geographic variations that differ from one another in small details, sometimes so slight that only a painstaking taxonomist making measurements with micrometer calipers or careful counts of body parts such as fin rays can tell them apart. In other cases the differences are great, not only in appearance but also in biology and habits.

The American Fisheries Society includes twenty-five species of fishes in the cod family, Gadidae, in its 1970 list. These fishes are found in the coastal waters of the continental shelf off the United States and Canada. The list includes such exotic-sounding forms as the toothed cod (*Arctogadus borisovi*), the cusk (*Brosme brosme*), the saffron cod (*Eleginus gracilis*), and the luminous hake (*Steindachneria argentea*).

The head of the clan is the Atlantic cod, *Gadus morhua morhua*. The group includes a number of subspecies, races, varieties, or hybrids. Six geographic subspecies are recognized by taxonomists, and for some of them the common names indicate where they are found. The Baltic

Close relatives of the cod include haddock and hake. Above, a haddock being hauled in hand over hand. Below, sorters at work in South Africa's hake fishery. (National Marine Fisheries Service, Albert C. Jensen)

cod (*Gadus morhua callarias*) is found in the Baltic Sea and nearby parts of the North Sea. The Kildin Island cod (*Gadus morhua kildinensis*) lives only in Lake Mogilno on Kildin Island in the Barents Sea. This lake is really a salt pond with salinity about twenty-two to twenty-three parts per thousand. Its bottom waters have high concentrations of hydrogen sulfide gas, and the Kildin Island cod is forced to live a mid-water instead of the normal bottom existence. The White Sea cod (*Gadus morhua maris-albi*) is found in the icy waters of the "sea" formed by the Arctic Ocean and the northern limits of the U.S.S.R. The White Sea winter cod (*Gadus morhua morhua natio hiemalis*) is a seasonal migrant into this area. This subspecies is so nearly like the type species that many experts doubt that it is really different from the Atlantic cod.

Two other fish ordinarily ranked as subspecies, the Greenland cod (*Gadus morhua ogac*) and the Pacific Cod (*Gadus morhua macrocephalus*), are regarded by some taxonomists as different enough to be considered separate species. The Pacific cod especially supports several fisheries.

The Greenland cod is very similar in form to the Atlantic cod, but it does not attain the massive size of its relative, growing only to a maximum of about twenty-two inches. The home range of the Greenland cod is the Arctic Ocean from West Greenland across the top of the world to Point Barrow, Alaska. It stays mostly in inlets and close to shore, only rarely going offshore and into deep water.

The Pacific or gray cod (*Gadus macrocephalus*) is caught in substantial numbers in the northern Pacific Ocean. In 1970, U.S. landings amounted to 2.8 million pounds, worth $179,000 to the fishermen. The U.S. Pacific cod fishery never was as large as that in the Atlantic; the record U.S. landings were made in 1915, when 32.7 million pounds were landed, which compared to 80.5 million pounds caught by U.S. fishermen in the Atlantic.

In appearance, habits, and the history of its exploitation the Pacific cod is very much like its Atlantic relative. The body is elongate and robust, and the head is large (hence the specific name, *macrocephalus*). It has the same three dorsal fins, the broad, somewhat spade-shaped tail fin, and the chin barbel. Its color is brown to gray on the upper surface and lighter on the lower surface, with numerous brown spots on the back and sides. It is a fast-growing fish, reaching a length of about ten inches after the first year, twenty inches after the second year, and twenty-four inches after the third year. By the end of the third year, the Pacific cod is sexually mature. It reaches a maximum length of three feet three inches, far less than the six feet of the Atlantic cod.

The Pacific cod is widely distributed around the great arc of the North Pacific from the Yellow Sea on the west coast of Korea to the California coast. The northern limit of its range is St. Lawrence Island in the Bering Sea off Alaska. It is intensely fished by several nations, with Japan taking about 69.5 per cent of the catch; the U.S.S.R., 19.5 per cent; the U.S., 5.7 per cent; Canada, 3.2 per cent; and South Korea, 2.1 per cent.

Pacific cod have long been important as food for aboriginal North Americans. Edgar O. Campbell, a schoolteacher on St. Lawrence Island in the Bering Sea, wrote in 1909 that the Eskimos would go off-shore in their "skin canoes" to fish, "but never more than a half mile from shore." In some years great numbers of cod were found frozen on the ice in November, and Campbell suggested that the fish "leaped up through the slushy sea ice and lay on top where they froze." As soon as the ice was solid enough to walk on, the Eskimos collected the fish and brought them into the villages to stack them in "great piles like cordwood."

The U.S. fishery for Pacific cod began in the 1860's. John N. Cobb, a member of the U.S. Fish Commission, wrote in 1916, "The first vessel to visit Bering Sea for cod was the schooner *Alert*, from San Francisco, in 1864. But little is known of this vessel and her owner or owners, but it is recorded that the venture was a failure, as only 9 tons of cod were secured."

Some of the first schooners of the Pacific cod fleet had been built in New England and sailed around Cape Horn to take part in the new fishery. Many of them even sailed 5,000 miles further to fish on the Asian side as far as the Okhotsk Sea, north of Japan, where the cod reached its greatest abundance. The fish were split and salted at sea, as in the Grand Bank fishery, and landed at San Francisco. This long-distance operation continued until 1884, when fishing grounds closer to home, in the southeastern Bering Sea and along the southern shore of Alaska, were exploited. The fishery here reached a peak in 1915, but because of economic problems it declined in 1933 and has remained at a low level. The present fishery is centered off the coasts of British Columbia and Washington.

One of the economic problems affecting the early Pacific cod fishery was a propaganda campaign waged in New England. Atlantic dealers had a firm grip on the East Coast and Middle West markets, and they had no intention of relinquishing even a small part to the salt cod from the Pacific. They spread the word that the western species is "not a true cod. It is an inferior fish that will not keep." As a result, Pacific cod processors had to look to Hawaii, Mexico, and the Asian countries for markets.

The Pacific cod played a part in American history, being one of the levers used to induce the United States government to negotiate with Russia for the acquisition of Alaska. A prime mover in the action was J. L. McDonald, a legislator in the territorial government of Washington. In a book, *Hidden Treasures, or Fisheries Around the Northwest Coast*, written in the late nineteenth century, he said: "In January, 1866, the author, while attending the session of the legislature at Olympia, the capital of Washington Territory, determined to make another bold push for Alaska by soliciting the good offices of our Government for the purpose of obtaining a permanent foothold and to open the prolific fishing grounds in those regions to our ambitious fishermen. To this end we penned the following memorial:"

To His Excellency Andrew Johnson, President of the United States:

Your memorialists, the legislative assembly of Washington Territory, beg leave to show that vast quantities of cod, halibut, and salmon of excellent quality are found along the shores of Russian America. Your memorialists respectfully request your Excellency to obtain such rights and privileges of the Government of Russia as will enable our fishing vessels to visit the harbors and its possessions, to the end that fuel, water, and provisions may be obtained; that our sick and disabled fishermen may obtain sanitary assistance, together with the privilege of taking and curing fish and repairing vessels in need of repairs. Your memorialists further request that the Secretary of the Treasury be instructed to forward to the collector of customs of this [Puget Sound] district, such fishing license, abstract journals, and log books as will enable our hardy fishermen to obtain the bounties now paid to the fishermen in the Atlantic states. Your memorialists finally pray your Excellency to employ such ships as may be spared from the Pacific naval fleet in surveying the fishing banks known to navigators to exist from the Cortez Bank to Bering Strait.

In his book, McDonald continued the account:

This memorial, written by a fisherman in behalf of the fishing industry on the northeast [west] coast, passed both branches of our Territorial legislature with commendable unanimity and dispatch. In forwarding a copy of the above-named memorial to the Secretary of State we imparted such information touching the fisheries around the Russian possessions, and the impulse which the opening of those resources to our fishermen would impart to the commercial development on the northwest coast. In acknowledging our humble services the illustrious Secretary assured us that "in consummating the recent purchase, I was strongly fortified by the letters which you wrote to me touching the valuable fisheries in those waters." The New York Times of April 1, 1867 (the acknowledged organ of Secretary Seward), said "that a memorial from the Territorial legislature of Washington Territory, dated January, 1866, asking the President to obtain certain rights for the fishermen, was the foundation of the present treaty."

On the 18th of October, 1867, the transfer of this vast territory from Russia to the United States was officially consummated at Sitka by the respective commissioners of the two Governments in the presence of the Russian population, who cheerfully welcomed the few Americans there also present. The union has been very cheerfully accepted by the people of the Territory. Our Government, on assuming possession, found numerous adventurers from the Pacific States domiciled in various parts of the Territory engaged in trade and in developing the resources in those regions; vessels laden with ware entered every harbor; stores were opened as by magic in every acceptable roadstead along the southern and western coasts; an active competition for furs, oil, ivory, old copper, iron, and junk was earnestly inaugurated; commerce revived, the sails of our vessels whitened every creek, bay, and sound, and the staid Russians very soon obtained an insight into Yankee progress on the go-ahead principle.

John N. Cobb of the U.S. Fish Commission wrote, "The acquisition of Alaska by the United States in 1867 proved an especial boon to our cod fishermen, as it secured them from any interference on the part of the Russians, who had not welcomed them very heartily in previous years."

The Russians had learned from the Eskimos how to catch cod for food and had depended on it when they first settled Alaska to exploit the fur resources. Modern Russians continue to use the Pacific cod for food, and are expanding their fisheries and introducing new fishing techniques.

In 1968, Soviet seiners in the Gulf of Anadyr caught an average of 250 tons of cod daily, but twenty vessels were often laid up because there were no carriers or factory vessels to collect the catches. According to *Vodnyi Transport* on July 25, 1968, the daily catches could have been increased to an average of 400 tons if mother ships had been available.

Besides the true cods of the genus *Gadus*, there are many other members of the cod family, resembling the patriarch to a greater or lesser degree in structure and habits.

The Arctic cod (*Boreogadus saida*) grows to a length of only six or eight inches. Found in the Arctic Sea from Greenland to Siberia, it is most common in the far north around Greenland and in Hudson Bay. In 1898, Drs. Jordan and Evermann reported in their monumental work *The Fishes of North and Middle America* the odd way in which they first collected specimens of the Arctic cod: "It was especially brought to our notice by its habit of hiding in small holes in the floating ice, from which it was dislodged by our steamer striking and turning over the blocks of ice. This floating ice was usually in 7 fathoms of water and 1 or 2 miles from the coast." They also collected specimens in a seine along northern beaches during the summer season when the shoreline was free of ice. Sometimes the fish stranded itself on the ice "by the hundreds" when it tried to escape the Beluga, or white whale.

Slender and streamlined, the Arctic cod resembles the pollock, another cod relative. R. A. McKenzie of the Fisheries Research Board of Canada, described an unusual collection of Arctic cod made in Miramichi Bay, which is far south of the usual range of the species. McKenzie speculated that a tongue of cold Arctic water had extended down into the bay. When a few Arctic cod were caught in a smelt trap

[43]

set beneath the ice, the local fishermen, who had never seen the fish before, thought that they were "just a queer sort of young cod fish with a forked tail and lower jaw stuck out beyond the upper." According to Dr. M. J. Dunbar of the Marine Sciences Center of McGill University, Montreal, the Arctic cod is "a High Arctic species of small abundance except very locally, and not worth considering for exploitation. The same is true of its cousin *Arctogadus glacialis* [polar cod]."

The polar cod may not be important for human food, but Norwegians have launched an experimental fishery to catch them for meal and oil. In 1969, the trade journal *News of Norway* reported that twenty to thirty boats were engaged in the fishery.

The pollock (*Pollachius virens*) is one of the most abundant of the cod relatives. This near-cod, a large, robust, streamlined fish, is also known as coal fish, saithe, and green cod. The name pollock is a modernized form of the old English *polog*, and has been Latinized to the scientific name of the genus.

The pollock does not look much like a cod. It is dark greenish-blue or greenish-gray with some silvery tints on the lower side, and has a spindle-shaped, well-streamlined body. The tail is distinctly forked, rather than broadly squared like the cod's. An adult pollock might be as much as three and a half feet long but it never grows to the large size attained by cod.

The pollock is almost always found in the mid-depths to upper layers of the water, unlike the cod, which ranges from the top to the bottom of the water column in its search for food. It feeds on a variety of organisms, especially young fishes. And Woods Hole biologists, examining pollock caught in the Gulf of Maine aboard the research vessel *Albatross III*, found the stomachs packed with the northern shrimp, *Pandalus borealis*. Pollock also gorge on other small shrimps, including *Meganyctiphanes* and *Thysanoessa*. *Pollachius* is common on both sides of the North Atlantic, and it is fished by a number of European countries, the United States, and Canada.

In the Pacific Ocean, the walleye or Alaska pollock (*Theragra chalcogramma*) is the chief prey of the fur seal. The United States catch of walleye pollock is relatively insignificant, amounting to less than 100,000 pounds annually, but it supports an important Japanese fishery in the Pacific. The U.N. Food and Agriculture Organization reports that in 1966 Japanese trawlers landed 774,800 metric tons (one metric ton equals 2,200 pounds) and the Soviet Union 425,200 metric tons. The Alaska pollock is a very popular fish on the Korean domestic market and the South Korean fishing industry has several large stern trawlers fishing in the North Pacific for the species.

In the North Atlantic, the most important cod relative is the haddock (*Melanogrammus aeglefinus*). Many European fisheries experts consider the haddock to be so closely related to the cod that they include it in the same genus, with the scientific name *Gadus aeglefinus*.

Haddock resemble cod in general body form but differ markedly in coloration. The most obvious difference is the haddock's black lateral line and black shoulder blotch, called "the devil's thumb print" or "St Peter's mark." The haddock is a dark purplish-gray on the top and sides, and silvery-gray toned with pink on the lower parts. Two rare color variations of the haddock have been reported: one, golden haddock, is a yellowish-bronze hue, almost a late-afternoon-sunshine tone; the other is serially striped, the fish being marked with a series of distinct vertical shaded bands. In eleven years of studying cod and haddock at Woods Hole, I saw only one golden haddock and never saw a striped one.

Mature haddock are between two and three feet long, and few live to be more than eleven or twelve years old. The largest haddock on record was an Icelandic fish forty-four inches long that weighed thirty-seven pounds. Maximum age is about 15 years.

The range of the haddock includes the waters off the coasts of northern Europe, the British Isles, and Iceland. In North American waters haddock are found off Newfoundland and Nova Scotia, in the Gulf of Maine, and on Georges Bank.

Haddock differ from cod in their food habits. The adults feed mostly on slow-moving small animals found on or burrowing in the upper layers of the ocean floor. Food items differ according to the type of bottom, but generally consist of crabs, shrimps, clams, snails, worms, starfish, sea urchins, sand dollars, and sea cucumbers. Haddock sometimes gorge themselves on burrowing worms grubbed out of the bottom. The haddock mouth is well suited to this type of feeding, and they have been called the "carp of the sea" because of their habit of rooting in the bottom for food. Fishes form only a small part of their diet, in contrast to the cod, but they occasionally feed on fish, mostly sand lance (*Ammodytes*) and squid.

The haddock fishery has been extremely important to both European and North American fishermen, but lately it has fallen on bad times. In the United States, for example, the annual landings of haddock once averaged about 100 million pounds. In the 1960's, for some as yet unexplained reason, the stocks of haddock on the banks off New England failed to reproduce themselves adequately. The last successful spawning was in the spring of 1963, and each succeeding year saw another failure. Adjusting to the smaller populations, the U.S. fishery maintained its level of harvest about equal to the annual crop of marketable haddock. In 1966, however, large fleets (up to 300 vessels) of Soviet trawlers began to exploit the haddock stocks of the New England banks. The combined effort of the relatively small U.S. fleet of trawlers and the massive Soviet armada proved too much for the haddock, especially those on Georges Bank. With very little reproduction to replace the removals by the fishing fleets, the actual number of haddock on the banks was reduced to the point where only a few large U.S. vessels found it profitable to continue the fishery. The Soviets shifted their effort to other species, especially mackerel (*Scombrus*) and yellowtail flounder (*Limanda*).

In an effort to restore the haddock, in 1969 the International Commission for the Northwest Atlantic Fisheries (ICNAF) established areas that were closed to fishing during February, March, and April (the haddock spawning season) for three years beginning in 1970. In addition to these closed areas, ICNAF also set a quota of 12,000 metric tons from ICNAF Subarea 5 (Georges Bank and the Gulf of Maine) as the total allowable catch for all nations that fish for haddock in this subarea. This is much less than the U.S. alone once landed.

Research showed that the available adult populations of Subarea 5 haddock at the beginning of 1970 was about 21 million fish, compared to the optimum of 145 million. With poor recruitment expected in 1970 and 1971, the annual quota of 12,000 metric tons would not allow improvement in stock size by 1972 unless recruitment in that year from the 1970 spawning is considerably improved.

The massive fleet of foreign trawlers off the coasts of the United States has also made serious inroads into the populations of other members of the cod family, the hakes. Soviet vessels exploited the silver hake (*Merluccius bilinearis*) on Georges Bank, the Atlantic hake (*M. albidus*) off the Middle Atlantic states and southward, and the Pacific hake (*M. productus*) off the west coast of the United States.

[46]

All three species of *Merluccius* resemble one another very closely. They are slender, streamlined fishes with well-developed teeth that enable them to catch and hold their prey—fish, squid, and shrimp.

The silver hake is one of the most abundant fishes of the Atlantic coastal waters. It is used as human food, for reduction to oil and meal, and for animal food, one of the few fishes used in so many ways.

There are ten hakes of the genus *Merluccius* found in many parts of the world ocean, off the coasts of Chile, England, South Africa, northwest Africa, and elsewhere. In 1961, I visited the South African hake fishery, centered in Cape Town. Large steel trawlers fish about fifty miles offshore for *Merluccius capensis*, which the South Africans call *stockfish*. Most of the catch is sold fresh but some of it is lightly smoked and appears in the fish shops under the name "finnan haddie." (True finnan haddie is lightly smoked haddock.) Any stockfish that is badly bruised or otherwise damaged on the trawler is culled from the catch ashore to be split, salted, and dried. The product is called "mine fish" and is shipped to the interior of the Republic of South Africa as food for the African laborers in the gold and diamond mines. Some of the mine fish formerly was sold to Nigeria, but that country no longer buys it, as a gesture of protest against South Africa's apartheid.

In addition to the hakes, there are a number of cod relatives, some locally important, some only ichthyological curiosities. The European whiting (*Gadus merlangus*) and the whiting pout (*Gadus luscus*) both contribute to the commercial landings of England and northern Europe; the poor cod (*Gadus nutus*) and the blue whiting (*Gadus poutassou*) are commercially insignificant.

Other cod relatives include the European lings (*Molva*), which may grow to five feet in length and are dried as stockfish in Iceland. In the northeastern United States the fish called ling is the red hake (*Urophycis chuss*), and is frequently caught by anglers from New York and New Jersey. Its larger relative, the white hake (*Urophycis tenuis*), is occasionally caught by New England trawlers while fishing for haddock and cod. White hake up to fifty pounds each are hooked and landed by anglers fishing the deep water between Nantucket Island and Montauk Point. A favorite "ground" is the wreck of the liner *Andrea Doria*, sunk in 200 fathoms.

In the early 1960's, red hake was used as the first raw material in experiments to develop a nutritious, protein-rich food additive called fish protein concentrate (FPC). Research at the Bureau of Commercial Fisheries Technological Laboratory at College Park, Maryland, showed that when the fish went through a grinding, solvent-extraction process it yielded a product at first called "fish flour." FPC is nearly white, flourlike, with neutral or faint taste and odor. Since it is nearly 80 per cent protein, it can be added in small amounts to foods ordinarily eaten in India, Africa, and other areas where the diets of the people are deficient in animal protein.

Red hake was chosen as the raw material because it is abundant off the U.S. east coast, it is underutilized as a food fish, and it is available for a considerable period during the year.

The Atlantic cod has only one freshwater relative, the burbot, lawyer, or ling (*Lota lota*). This is a slender fish, unlike the robust cod, but it does have the prominent barbel or chin whisker that sets it aside from any other freshwater species. The body coloration is olive to dark greenish brown above with dark mottlings, fading to a dusky gray below. Burbots as large as thirty inches long have been caught, but the average size is about fifteen inches long and one pound in weight. The type species, *Lota lota lota*, occurs in the northern parts of Eurasia. The American subspecies, *Lota lota maculosa*, is common in many lakes (including the Great Lakes) in Minnesota, Iowa, the north-central states, and south-central Canada. Both anglers and commercial fishermen land the burbot, and although the flesh is said to be strong-flavored, it is widely accepted as a food fish. James R. Harland and Everett B. Speaker of the Iowa State Conservation Commission report that at one time the large, oily livers of the burbot were extracted for medicinal purposes. Another burbot subspecies, *Lota lota leptura*, occurs in the Yukon River region, and in other waters in Alaska and northeastern Siberia.

One cod relative, the tomcod, is the bane of students of marine ichthyology. There are two species: the Pacific tomcod (*Microgadus proximus*), occurring from California northward to Alaskan waters, and the Atlantic tomcod (*Microgadus tomcod*). Most adult tomcods are less than a foot long but they look very much like the Atlantic cod. Dr. Henry B. Bigelow and William C. Schroeder, Woods Hole Oceanographic Institution scientists, say, "The tomcod resembles a small cod so closely in its fins, in the projection of its upper jaw beyond the lower, in the presence of a barbel on its chin; and in its pale lateral line, that the one might easily be taken for the other."

Both species of tomcod live in shallow water along the coast. The

Atlantic tomcod is considered both a marine and a freshwater fish, migrating into many east coast estuaries in the fall and winter to spawn.

Despite their diminutive size, tomcod are favorites with anglers, who catch them from piers and bridges and in salt creeks, in midsummer and in winter. When they catch them in the cold months, New York and New Jersey anglers call them "frost fish." They also call silver hake frost fish since these are also caught from piers and bridges in the winter, and this leads to confusion.

Both kinds of tomcod are delicious, but they are never abundant enough to make a sizable contribution to the market. In the 1850's, between 5,000 and 10,000 pounds were caught annually in the Charles River near Boston, Massachusetts. As late as 1942, 37,500 pounds of Atlantic tomcod were caught for the market. In recent years, however, the catch has been so small that it is not even reported in the fisheries statistics. In contrast, the Pacific tomcod continues to be landed by commercial fishermen, and the National Marine Fisheries Service reports that 162,000 pounds of Pacific tomcod, worth $1,600 to the fishermen, were caught in 1970.

The success of the fisheries for cod and for some of their relatives encouraged the marketing of a veritable host of "false cods," in most cases fish not even distantly related to the Atlantic cod. Six species found off the Pacific coast of North America called cod are mostly of the scorpion fish family, Scorpaenidae, which includes the valuable redfish or ocean perch (*Sebastes*). Among these species are the black cod, now called sablefish (*Anoplopoma fimbria*), the blue or bull cod (cabezon—*Scorpaenichthys marmoratus*), the channel cod (thornyhead—*Sebastolobus altivelis*), the chili cod (chilipepper—*Sebastes goodei*), and the rock cod (rockfish—*Sebastes*). The only one of the false cods still known by a common name that includes the word cod is the lingcod, or cultus cod (*Ophiodon elongatus*). The sablefish and the lingcod each contribute millions of pounds annually to the landings from the Pacific and Bering Sea.

At the other end of the world, the Soviets are starting an Antarctic fishery for a little known species of false cod, *Notothenia* (*guntheri?*), that belongs to the perch family, Percidae. It is a cold-water species that can not survive temperatures above about 43 degrees Fahrenheit, lives at depths of about 150 fathoms, and has an average length of twenty-three to thirty-one inches. It is said to have a delicate flavor.

The Soviet trade journal *Vodnyi Transport* reports that the fishery is conducted by vessels of the Murmansk trawler fleet under the Soviet Northern Fisheries Administration. These vessels were joined by the factory trawler *Skazochnik Andersen*, a ship of about 4,700 gross tons, whose catches average ten to twenty metric tons per haul.

The abundance, variety of species, and excellent food value of the cod family were factors that led the fishing industry to give the name to the false cods to make them more acceptable to consumers. But the false cods are not at all as important on the world market as the true cods. The members of the cod family are second only to the herring family, Clupeidae, in volume of commercial landings. In 1969 (most recent data available), the world catch of clupeids was 40.3 billion pounds while the catch of gadids was 21.7 billion pounds. By far, the majority of the cod, haddock, hakes, etc. are used directly for human food. In contrast, many of the herrings, especially the menhaden and anchoveta, are used as industrial fish, for oil and meal.

5

The Beef of the Sea

MAN IS AN OMNIVOROUS ANIMAL, but eagerly seeks his protein food from animal flesh. Very early in his development, man probably found fish to be one of the most easily accessible sources of animal protein, and he caught them with traps, spears, and crude angling devices in lakes, ponds, and streams. For example, Dr. Sándor Bökönyi, Curator of the Hungarian National Museum in Budapest, reports that fish bones made up nearly 60 per cent of the remains in a Neolithic kitchen midden he examined in the northern Balkans which dated back almost 7,000 years. Deer bones made up 27 per cent of the remains while the rest included those of wild cattle and horses. As the human populations grew, coastal tribes and wanderers from the interior who reached the sea soon discovered that here was a veritable storehouse of fishes in great abundance.

It is a safe assumption that in the days before the Christian era, the dwellers of the fens of the north country—Scotland and Scandinavia—included cod in their diet. Most of the fish they caught and ate were those that were easy to catch in quantity. Salmon in the rivers and perhaps flounder in the shallow bays made up the bulk of the ancient fisheries. But cod also probably blundered into the crude traps set in the bays or came close enough to shore to be speared or caught on primitive hooks or gorges. Even today, many anglers catch cod while fishing from the shore. Each spring, hundreds of cod weighing up to thirty-five pounds are caught from the banks of the Cape

Deckload of cod aboard West German trawler on Grand Bank. (National Marine Fisheries Service)

Cod Canal in Massachusetts. The cod pursue the springtime schools of spawning alewives, a small herringlike fish, and are caught by anglers using alewives for bait. And cod still blunder into the traps set within a few hundred yards of the shoreline off Newfoundland, New England, and Long Island.

To exploit the real wealth of the sea, however, the early fishermen had to develop sturdy boats that would carry them a mile or so offshore. In the deep, mysterious waters they found herring in great abundance, and the cod. Both species were well suited to salting and drying for storage and use during the winter months when the sea proved most inhospitable.

At first, for cod at least, any surplus fish probably were preserved for later use by simply drying them in the sun and wind. Dr. C. L. Cutting, the British fisheries expert, points out that the control of fire led to cooking and then to artificial drying of fish and meat by exposure to the heat and smoke of burning wood. The smoke also helped to keep flies off the fish as it dried over the fires, and at one time wood ashes also were used to help preserve the dried fish. It is possible this was a lucky discovery when some fish fell into the ashes of a smoking fire and it was found that the ash-covered fish lasted longer when dried. The discovery of mineral salt, however, quickly led to salting and drying as a better way to preserve the fish.

As the early Europeans evolved from a hunting and gathering society to an agrarian society, fishing assumed a lesser role as a source of protein food. Richard Lewinsohn, the German historian and philosopher, has said that fishing did not develop the significance in Europe that it did in Asia. He cites as an example that in India and Ceylon fish hooks were the most ancient form of money, demonstrating the importance of the art of fishing. Nevertheless, fish was a more important food than red meat for millions of people in Europe. The great majority of the coastal population lived from the products of the fisheries, and trade in fishes was one of the few branches of European economy that was organized on an international basis at the start of the Middle Ages (about 476 to 1500).

The main species in this early medieval trade was herring. Sweden supplied half of Europe with the salt herring required for the Lenten season. Then the cities of the Hanseatic league seized control of the herring trade.

Early in the sixteenth century, the herring fishery on which the

Hansa depended collapsed. The fish simply were not available to the fishermen, and even today biologists are not able to explain whether it was capricious ocean currents, a virulent disease, or overpredation by cod and other fishes that caused the catastrophe. It was a terrible economic blow to the industry and fishermen looked to an alternate species—cod.

Cod were already well known to the Hansa merchants; in Norway, they had long traded stockfish and cod-liver oil. The cod came from the Lofoten Islands fishery, where cold but sunny and dry spring weather was well suited to making stockfish.

The disappearance of the herring and the substitution of cod in the Lenten fasting meals fostered daring, long-ranging exploration of the northern seas. The impetus for these journeys was quite simple: the scarcity of fish was followed by a steep rise in prices, and the demand for fish of any kind was so great that it was profitable to send the fishing fleets out to distant waters. Many historians believe that this situation provided the spark that eventually helped to get the Newfoundland fisheries underway.

Long before the herring failure, however, European ships had sailed to distant seas for fish. Seamen from English east coast ports first reached Iceland in the twelfth century. They had followed flocks of birds to rediscover this northerly island and its abundance of herring and cod. (Vikings had been there 200 years before.) Incredibly, these twelfth-century fishing vessels were merely large rowing boats with fourteen to twenty-six oars and a single square sail to set when the wind was favorable. The ship resembled the one we know today as the dragon ship of the Vikings.

This distant water fishery profited so well that by the thirteenth century English fishermen annually sent twenty ships to Iceland and the northern sea. These vessels were "doggers," two-masted ketches that were superior to the earlier "Icelandic ship," which could fish a greater distance from shore and also used "long lines with many hooks." The English fleets were so efficient that the Icelanders complained that the English were decimating the cod populations. One dogger could carry five or ten men with the summer's provisions and salt for the catch and return with "fifteen lasts" (about thirty tons) of fish. The fleet left England in February or March, and with favorable winds and weather reached Iceland in about a week. The ships fished all summer, with occasional visits to England to unload the catch and return. The split salt cod was sold in England during October and November to be stored for Lent. It could be safely kept for up to two years if put under a thick layer of straw and covered with mats to keep it dry.

It is difficult today to imagine what the life of these fishermen must have been like. Their journey to the Icelandic fishing grounds began at a time when that part of the North Atlantic was still in the frigid grasp of winter. There was no protection on the undecked vessel; the men were exposed to wintry blasts from the Arctic, chilled by the waves and spray that came over the rail of the tiny boat, and during the too-brief summer they were broiled by the glaring sun. But cod was needed for the Lenten days of fast, and so they fished.

The offshore fisheries supplied the salt-fish market while the coastal fisheries continued to supply the fresh-fish market. It was a problem, however, to deliver fresh fish to important inland markets such as London and Paris. To protect the populace from the sale of spoiled sea food, regulations were established to control their sale. Thus, in the time of Edward I (1272–1307) no fish, unless it was salted, could be kept in London beyond the second day. At the time, salted and smoked fish were cheaper than fresh fish because of the difficulties of transport and the risks that had to be taken with the fresh product. In 1298, "large stockfisshe" were a penny each in London. The prices demanded for fresh fish put it well beyond the reach of the majority of the population and so they bought the dried or salted and dried product.

Air-dried cod and dried salted cod have two fine qualities that endeared them to naval and military commanders several centuries ago —they take up comparatively little space for the amount of edible material available, and they keep well on long journeys. Thus, much to the disgust of the men in the ranks, it was a constant provision of armies and navies of the time. In 1281, when Edward I raised an army to invade Wales, he commissioned "one Adam of Fulsham," an Alderman of London, to buy pickled fish, including 5,000 salt cod in Aberdeen, Scotland. C. L. Cutting also relates that dried and salt cod—along with salt beef and pork—became the standby of the Elizabethan mariner. Thus, two of the Virgin Queen's admirals saw to it that their jolly tars did not lack for cod while on the high seas. Hawkins, in

1564, shipped six lasts (about twelve tons) of stockfish. In 1577, another mariner, Frobisher, included two and a half tons of stockfish in his ship's stores.

The seaman's dependence on dried salt cod soon caused it to be known as the "beef of the sea," a name that persisted into the twentieth century. The fish made it possible for vessels to range well into the tropics and thus it played a part in the explorations of Spain and Portugal in the New World. About 1650, it was said, "neither can the Hollanders Spaniards or Portugals well get any ship to the Indies without Newfoundland fish, there being no fish that will endure to pass the line [the Equator] sound and untainted but the fish of that country salted and dried there."

And how was the product received by its consumer? What did the dried salt cod of the sixteenth century taste like? We can get some idea of the appreciation held for the beef of the sea from the writings of Thomas Nashe, a British author of the time. In 1592, Nashe wrote a treatise entitled "Pierce Penilesse His Supplication to the Divell," in which he describes a spendthrift law student who goes to sea in hopes of replenishing his fortune.

> Poore soule he lyes in brine in Balist, and is lamentable sicke of the scurvies, his dainty fare is turned to a hungry feast of Dogs and Cats, or Haberdine [large salt cod] and poore Iohn [Poor John, the smallest salt cod from Newfoundland] at the most, and which is lamentablest of all, that without Mustard. . . . It is a pleasante thing ouer a full pot, to read the fable of thirsty Tantalus: but a harder matter to digest salt meates at Sea, with stinking water.

It is not quite clear how the mustard would have improved the flavor of the "poore soule's" diet except perhaps to have masked it, but certainly the taste of the mustard would not have improved the "stinking water." If anything, it would have made the desperate and unhappy would-be seaman thirstier still.

Of course there were other potable liquids aboard the ships besides water. Typical shipboard provisions of the time included beer, cider, and malmsey. Any such journey must have been a thirst-provoking one. What little fluid remained in the seaman's system after a meal of salt fish or beef would surely have been removed by the alcohol in the beer, the cider, and the sweet malmsey wine. We can easily sympathize with Nashe's hapless law student.

Although stockfish and dried salt cod were not held in high esteem by their consumers, they were nevertheless important as food and kept the various national fisheries flourishing for centuries. And aboard ship, the thrifty fishermen made it a practice also to save whatever else of the cod that could be put to some use. The cod tongues saved by each fisherman as a tally of his daily catch were salted in barrels and returned ashore. The muscular tongues have a distinctive and pleasant flavor and even today are considered a delicacy when dipped in batter and fried.

In addition to the tongues, the air bladders, or "sounds," were preserved in salt. The tough, membraneous sounds yield a high-quality gelatin (isinglass) that was commonly used for making glue and jelly and as a thickening agent in cooking. Vintners and brewers used the isinglass to settle sediment in their beverages and clarify them. Cod sounds to be made into isinglass were saved as part of the catch even into the early twentieth century.

Fishermen on the Brittany coast used salted cod eggs as a "chum" to attract pilchards. Most highly prized were the full, ripe ovaries that were collected in the fall and early winter. At this season, the mature females were preparing to spawn, and these ovaries yielded the most and largest eggs.

The fishermen of the sixteenth century also began to save the cod livers. These too were placed in barrels aboard ship, without salt, and allowed to rot so that the rich, honey-colored oil separated from the tissues and floated to the top. A visitor to Iceland in 1563 described the method then in use ashore to extract the oil: "Having taken them [cod] they plucke out the bones, and lay up their bowels, and make Fat or Oyle of them." Cod-liver oil was in great demand by tanners and for quite some time they were the only users. Its pharmaceutical properties were not recognized until much later.

Cod-liver oil was second only to stockfish as an important product of the Hanseatic league. The product was dark-colored and evil-smelling and was used not only by tanners but also in oil lamps. It was called "train oil," said to be a corruption of the term, "*trän* oil," from the Germanic word *tränen* (tears). This was in reference to the "tears" of oil that dripped from the rotting livers. The train oil lamps were black iron trays with a wick hanging out at each corner; they gave out only a pale light, smoked badly, and must have smelled abominably.

The first medicinal use of cod-liver oil probably was rooted in the natureopathic philosophy that leads many people to use almost any "natural" substance as a remedy of sorts. Many rural Americans, for example, used turpentine (derived from pine trees) and kerosene as liniments following the idea that natural products were somehow mysteriously beneficial to health. Perhaps the early fishermen rubbed the cod-liver oil on their hands to soothe the sores and chafing caused by handling fishing lines. Eventually it probably followed that this natural product could also be taken internally. As early as 1770, people in North Atlantic ports were experimenting with it as a food supplement for the sick and the aged. Any modern parent who has ever tried to get his children to take the highly refined cod-liver oil (sometimes flavored with peppermint) available today can well imagine what it must have been like to swallow a dose of the oil of two centuries ago. Two British researchers, Drs. J. C. Drummond and T. P. Hilditch, said the oil was "deep golden brown in colour, [and] possessed a highly objectionable flavour and a strong fishy smell."

Clinical evaluation of cod-liver oil in the treatment of certain bone infections was carried on by Dr. Samuel Kay between 1752 and 1784 at the Manchester, England, infirmary. In 1822, a Dr. Schrenk of Germany published the results of his experimental use of cod-liver oil as a therapeutic agent. The oil was in general use throughout western Europe in the treatment of rickets, a new malady affecting city children. By 1840, this led to the search for more efficient ways of producing the oil and also of producing one more palatable. An effective process was soon invented by Charles Fox of Scarborough, England.

Scarborough was a fishing port for the newly developed North Sea trawl fishery but apparently the supply of cod livers was not to Fox's liking, for he migrated to St. John's, Newfoundland. In 1848, Fox introduced his new method for extracting the oil. Instead of letting the livers rot, Fox heated them in pans jacketed with hot water or steam. He chose only livers in good condition and removed the gall bladders, which imparted a bitter taste to the oil. The oil he produced was lighter in color than the oil from the rotted livers and many people considered it "weaker" and inferior to the dark oils. Soon after the middle of the nineteenth century, however, the rotting method of producing cod liver had almost completely disappeared. Today, factory trawlers produce crude cod-liver oil at sea by direct steam injection into pans of the livers. The oil then is returned to factories ashore for further refining.

Cod-liver oil remained in use as a general tonic, but not until 1921, when biochemist E. V. McCallum proved its value, was it clearly recognized as a specific cure for rickets. Later research showed its action was due to vitamins A and D, and vitamin D was the "sunshine" vitamin. Cod-liver oil—sunshine from the sea—became a common household remedy.

There are still some adherents to the rotted-liver method of making crude cod-liver oil. In 1955, I was aboard the research vessel *Albatross III* on Georges Bank. During the course of the cruise we took a number of cod, and the ship's Chief Engineer, Franklin Macaulay, carefully saved about a gallon of the livers. He put them in a large open can in a warm part of the engine room to let the livers rot. It was not long before the distinctive smell of the rotting mass permeated the engine room, the galley, the mess, and the scientists' sleeping quarters. Mr. Macaulay never got to use his cod-liver oil, however. One dark night when the Chief Engineer was off watch and asleep, someone took the can and its odoriferous contents and consigned it to the legendary Davy Jones's locker.

Despite the distinctive taste and aroma which even modern technology has not been able to entirely eliminate, cod-liver oil is still very much sought after. In the U.S. Pharmacopoeia (USP) it is known as Oleum Morrhuae, and is described as a readily digested fat that is rich in A and D vitamins. USP cod-liver oil must contain at least 850 USP units of vitamin A and 85 USP units of vitamin D in each gram.

The oil is dispensed in a variety of liquids, emulsions, and capsules for ease of administration as a vitamin supplement. It is also sold in liquid form, often flavored to mask the distinctive taste and aroma. The oil has even been included in salves and ointments for the treatment of burns and other skin wounds. However, recent research by a team of U.S. Bureau of Commercial Fisheries chemists, led by Dr. Maurice E. Stansby, led them to conclude that cod-liver oil "failed to promote healing to any greater extent than did mineral oil applied in the same manner."

The current world demand for cod-liver oil remains high and is supplied largely by the nations that also supply large volumes of cod in its various forms for food. In recent years, Norway exported 44 million pounds of oil per year and Iceland exported 10 million pounds.

Cod was, and is, pre-eminent on the world market as a desirable, nutritious food product. In a report on the food values of fish, Andrew W. Anderson, Assistant Director of the U.S. Bureau of Commercial Fisheries, reports that cod is high in protein (about 18 per cent), low in fat (less than 1 per cent), and about 85 to 95 per cent digestible. Dried cod (stockfish) and dried salt cod contain all the food nutrients of the fresh fish but less than half the moisture, which, in the fresh fish, amounts to about 67 per cent.

Our present-day knowledge of the nutritive value of cod is based on modern research in well-equipped laboratories, but in earlier times physicians and others had to rely solely on their observations or, often, intuitively derived opinions of the product. In 1753, Dr. S. Nelson, a British physician prepared "An Essay on the Government of Children," in which he said, "Fish is a sort of Diet extremely improper for Children. I would recommend to Parents never to let a Child so much as taste it for the first seven years at least." The salted and dried fish available at the time, according to another writer, "are left in a condition that demands the greatest efforts by the stomach to extract the food value from the fibrous masses."

A startling opportunity to actually watch human digestion of cod came as the result of an accident at Mackinac, Michigan, in 1822. Alexis St. Martin, a nineteen-year-old Canadian, was injured by a shotgun blast that tore away part of his chest including a portion of the stomach wall. The young trapper was treated by the trading post physician, Dr. William Beaumont. The boy recovered but the gaping wound never completely healed so that he literally had a stomach with a window in it.

Dr. Beaumont took the opportunity to watch the action of digestion on various foods eaten by St. Martin and later reported his observations in a scientific paper titled "Experiments and Observations on the Gastric Juice," published in 1838. His report recorded the digestibility of codfish eaten by Alexis St. Martin and compared it to other foods he ate:

> April 9th [1830]. At 3 o'clock P.M. he dined on boiled, dried codfish, potatoes, parsnips, bread and butter. [At 3:30 P.M.] I examined him and took out a portion; it was about half digested, the potatoes the least so of any part of the dinner. The fish was broken down into small filaments. . . .

At 4 o'clock I examined another portion. Digestion had regularly advanced, and very few particles of fish remained entire. Some of the few potatoes were distinctly to be seen.

Dr. Beaumont's experiments proved the digestibility of cod, but it was the abundance, long storage life, and availability to the consumer, not its nutritive value, that made dried salt cod and stockfish the mainstay of much of the population of the western hemisphere. But this was all to change as the new science of food technology developed in the late nineteenth century.

People who lived near the shore were accustomed to fresh fish from the inshore boat and trap fisheries but everyone else had to be content with the dried and salted product. As one modern economist stated, "Considering the quality of the fish they had to eat, it is no wonder it was considered a penance food." Even the preparation of the fish for the family table was something of an ordeal. A nineteenth-century housewife who wanted to prepare a codfish dinner was advised to "lay the fish into the cellar a few days before it is to be cooked, that it may be softened by the dampness. The afternoon before it is to be boiled, wash it carefully in several waters. It is well to keep a brush on purpose to cleanse salt fish and use it repeatedly while it is soaking."

When the opportunity was presented to her, the nineteenth-century housewife was only too happy to take advantage of the supply of fresh or only lightly salted fish. The newer products were offered by merchants in place of the board-hard slabs of cod she was accustomed to. In part, the change in type of fish available (salt cod versus fresh cod) was brought about by technological developments in other fields, and improvements in transportation played a big part in the change.

The development and improvement of railroads and, later, motor trucks changed the whole picture of fish distribution. As fresh fish became more readily available through better distribution, consumer demand increased. A preference for less salty products developed and the industry responded with lighter salting and softer drying. This, of course, meant the fish was more perishable and had to be distributed and consumed as quickly as possible.

Cod taken near the shore in traps could be more lightly salted than cod taken on the banks, which required plenty of salt to keep them until they could be landed. This led to greater use of cod traps, great net enclosures with a simple entrance and no real exit, especially in areas where high humidity and lack of sunshine made drying conditions bad. Labrador is such an area, and fish cured there produced a lightly salted fish used for "boneless cod," the trade name for cured cod in which the skin and bones are removed and the fish is cut in pieces three to eight inches long.

It was not long, either, before icing fish at sea became more common and in some markets, particularly the United States, demand for cod declined as fresh haddock and other fish became more popular.

At first, neither fisherman nor their customers fully accepted iced fish. The fishermen believed that ice in contact with the fish adulterated and ruined the flesh as the melting ice dripped through the catch in the hold. The consumers believed that iced fish must have been spoiled to begin with and that the ice was being used to prevent further deterioration. This same sort of belief is prevalent in some areas today. Mr. R. Hamlisch and Dr. R. A. Taylor, writing in the United Nations Food and Agriculture Organization publication "Fish in Nutrition," mention that in the African nation of Uganda consumers are not willing to buy frozen fish, even when fresh fish are scarce and of doubtful quality. The Africans explain that "only 'bad' fish are frozen, that frozen fish spoil very quickly, and they do not like 'hard' fish because they can not judge its quality in the familiar way."

As technological changes gave the consumer a greater variety of fish products to choose from, sociological changes acted to influence his choice. Hamlisch and Taylor say, "The make-up of fish consumption has been changing in many European countries. In general, there has been a decline in the demand for salted and dried products and for cheaper fresh fish in the northern European countries. . . . In Spain, Portugal, and southern European countries, on the other hand, per capita consumption of salted fish has risen appreciably over the last decade."

The reasons behind these differences in consumption are relatively simple. For one thing, the various European countries are at different stages of economic development. In the higher-income countries the consumer is able to afford the better quality, more desired fresh cod. In the lower-income and less developed countries, particularly in southern Europe, lack of refrigeration and freezer facilities and less available cash force the consumer to continue to buy salted dried cod. Italy is the principal European market for stockfish, and most of it is sold in Venice, Sicily, and Naples. In the industrial north of Italy, the market favors heavily salted fish, whereas in the agricultural south of Italy, the market favors lightly salted but hard-dried fish.

Dr. Francisco Lopez Capont of Vigo, describing the fisheries of Spain, reports: "All cod eaten in Spain is salted and dried. Efforts to promote fresh fillets have failed. Dried and salted cod (bacalao) constitutes a popular food consumed in large quantities throughout the entire year with a natural increase in the winter. In many regions of Spain cod tongues constitute a typical dish."

In a country such as Norway, if he is willing, the consumer can eat cod every day of the week, served a different way each time. I found this out during a visit to Bergen to attend a scientific meeting a few years ago. My wife came with me, and to help our budget we ate "on the economy." We had our evening meal in a small restaurant that catered to what seemed to us to be the workingman of Bergen. One night we had boiled cod served with a white sauce and boiled potatoes. The next night it was boiled salt cod served with a sauce made from the cod livers boiled in vinegar water. The night after we had steamed cod fillets, again with boiled potatoes. The following night the feature on the menu was *fiskesuppe* (fish soup) made with cod. We found red meat to be expensive and scarce in our little cafe, probably beyond the average workingman's pocketbook. Although ham was also on the menu, the servings were small compared to the amounts of cod served. The potatoes were delicious but the only other vegetables available were cabbage (plentiful), carrots (scarce), and peas (rare).

A demand for salt cod still exists in many of the tropical countries of Africa, South and Central America, and the islands of the Caribbean. (Many of those same islands had been part of the sugar-rum producing complex where the slaves had been fed salt New England cod.) Here in the hot, humid climate, perspiration losses of body salt make additional salt intake a necessity.

On the other hand, some tropical nations prefer nonsalted fish and may reject salted fish outright. Thus in Ghana, Nigeria, and among the Bantu in the Congo there is almost no demand for salt fish. Some dealers have found it is often difficult to make consumers in these nations accept even a slightly salted fish product. But the same consumers eagerly accept the air-dried cod. The nation of Nigeria on the Gulf of Guinea, just north of the Equator, is an important market for stockfish, especially from Norway and Iceland. In a recent year, Norway exported 54 million pounds of stockfish to Nigeria, and Iceland exported

18 million pounds. But the political unrest in Africa has had considerable impact on the market for cod.

The recent civil war in Nigeria seriously affected one of Iceland's important stockfish markets. The greatest percentage of the air-dried cod produced by this North Atlantic island was sold to Nigeria, a substantial amount to Italy, and a little to Sweden. In 1966, Iceland sold a total of 8,217 metric tons to Nigeria, while in 1967 the amount was only 2,188 metric tons.

As a result of this loss of market, there is a considerable accumulation of unsold stockfish in Iceland. Stocks in recent years amount to between 6,300 and 6,600 metric tons. The Icelandic stockfish producers asked their government for help, since they have to pay interest on loans in addition to large storage costs for the unsold stocks. To complicate matters, the producers had no way of knowing when, or at what price, they would be able to dispose of the stockfish in storage. An attempt has been made to find new markets for Icelandic stockfish in other African states, but so far these efforts have met with little success. Part of the problem is that many of the African coastal nations are establishing their own ocean fisheries and thus producing supplies of fresh fish. Some of the African markets, too, have long been supplied by the export production of the Republic of South Africa.

As we have seen, the United States is a good market for cod produced by the fisheries of other nations, especially frozen cod blocks, which are the raw material for fish sticks, a product that revolutionized the fish processing industry as a convenience food. A fish stick is officially defined as "an elongated piece of fish flesh (generally cut from a block of fillets) weighing not less than three-quarters of an ounce and not more than one and a quarter ounces with the largest dimension at least three times that of the next largest dimension." The usual dimensions are three inches long, a half inch wide, and three-eighths of an inch deep. The sticks are sawed with a band saw from a block of frozen cod fillets that is about two feet long, one and a half feet wide, and six inches deep. The sticks, still frozen, go onto a conveyer belt and pass through a batter and tumble into a breading mixture. From the mixture the sticks are deep-fried, packaged, and frozen. The housewife has only to heat the fish sticks and serve them.

Fish sticks were developed in the United States in the early 1950's, and two years later production zoomed to 50 million pounds annually. In 1970 production amounted to a record 116 million pounds. Fish sticks are very popular in other parts of the world as well. In England they found a ready market and are as well received there as in the United States. Other products cut from the frozen cod blocks include fish portions—square "patties" that are popular in the quick-lunch and hot-fish sandwich trade.

As we approach the final quarter of the twentieth century, it is obvious that cod does not occupy the same position it held in earlier centuries. It is no longer largely a penance food, to be eaten as a demonstration of denial on religious fast days. Instead, it is eagerly sought for its own sake as a high-quality, nutritious, tasty food product. And as the world human population grows, the demand for cod—along with other fish products—also will grow.

The U.S. per capita consumption of fish today is 11.2 pounds annually, of which about one pound is cod. In Great Britain, however, the annual per capita consumption of fish is twenty-one pounds, while in Iceland it is a whopping eighty-six pounds, probably the highest in the world, and much of it cod. To satisfy the demand of her home markets and provide enough cod for export, Great Britain's trawlers must land more than 774 million pounds of cod annually. Icelandic trawlers must land more than 678 million pounds of cod each year to satisfy home and export market demands. Canadian fishermen land more than 578 million pounds of cod, but most of this is exported (and the greatest portion to the United States) since Canada's per capita consumption is only fourteen pounds per year. Thus, it is evident that the world demand for cod has grown over the centuries, and because world population has grown the annual landings figures for cod today approach astronomical proportions. And, based on a billion individual cod landed each year, the actual numbers of cod in the ocean must also be astronomical. The day may be coming soon when the demand may very well equal the actual number of cod available.

Modern trawlers: Above, a large steel otter trawler of the type that fishes out of Boston; below, a Soviet factory stern trawler hauling back its otter trawl on Georges Bank. (National Marine Fisheries Service)

6

Development of the World Cod Fishery

ENGLAND'S CENTURIES-LONG DOMINATION of the seas was early helped by two unrelated industries—textile manufacture and fishing. As the textile industry expanded, England's population expanded as well. More cloth became available for export, and English merchants went farther abroad seeking markets for the products of the cottagers' labor. The expanding population also strained the ability of the English fishermen to satisfy the demand for fish. Thus, the fishermen went farther abroad seeking other sources of cod. During the fourteenth century, stockfish imports were increased from the Netherlands and Norway to help fill the demand, and English fishermen joined their Scandinavian neighbors in fishing off the coasts of Denmark and Norway as far north as the Lofoten Islands.

While the English made stockfish, the French in the New World also were fishing for cod, but the large cod the French caught on the Grand Bank were too thick for stockfish and had to be carefully salted. The French vessels of this early Grand Bank fishery were about 100 tons burden, with space for a crew of fifteen to eighteen men and food and supplies to last six months. The men fished from the deck of the vessel with handlines and usually caught between twenty-five and 200 cod daily. Sometimes, when the fish were especially abundant the daily catch per man would be as much as 350 to 400 fish. At the end of the day the catch was dressed and salted down below decks.

The salting process was most critical because it made the difference between a boatload of half rotten or rock-hard fish and a load of well-preserved fish that would bring a good price at home. Thus the salter was the key man in the operation, and among other things he had to know how to test the strength of the salt. Because of the vagaries of the weather during the making of solar salt, the final product varied greatly in quality. The salter had to know at a glance how much salt each fish required and on what part of the split carcass the most salt was needed for best preservation. Any mistake and the fish either came out "slack" and strong-smelling from too little salt or "dry as a chip" from oversalting.

The French practice for preparing the cod from the Cape Breton fishery centered around four specialists: the *piquer* or "throater," who slit the throat and belly of the fish to let it bleed and to permit evisceration; the *decoleur* or "header," who cut off the head; the *trancheur* or "splitter," who opened the carcass to the familiar butterfly shape and removed the forward part of the backbone; and finally the *saleur* or "salter." Working below decks, the salter built up a bed of salted fish —one layer of salt, one of cod—nine to ten feet long and three feet high with the fish placed flesh side up. The cod remained in "salt bulk" for five or six days and then were washed in sea water to remove the excess salt. They were piled to drain off the water and then spread on the rocky beach (later, on crude wooden racks or "flakes") to dry, flesh side up during the day, skin side up during the night or in damp weather. After the fish were judged to be properly dry, they were piled to "sweat" for a month before loading into the ship for return to Europe. As much as 300 quintals (a quintal equals 100 pounds) of cod would be put in one pile, which helped to further flatten the fish and literally squeeze out much of the remaining moisture.

The great demand for salt to preserve fish had some far-reaching ecological and sociological side effects. In eleventh-century Britain, for example, salt was obtained by evaporating sea water. In the summer it was made in great metal pans heated by the sun, but in the winter the water had to be heated artificially. The ruthless use of wood for fuel to boil the salt pans has been blamed for the destruction of English forests. As wood became scarce the salt makers used coal, another of Britain's natural resources, and it was not long before coal mining and salt panning became closely linked. Coal miners and salt panners in Scotland existed in conditions of abject slavery, with women and children as well as men laboring long hours in the dark confines of the mine galleries. Many of the women were harnessed to pull mine carts filled with coal and did the work of pit ponies. The children often picked over the coal to separate the fuel from slate and other rocks. It was not until the Act of 1799 that the coal miners and salt panners were emancipated from their near slavery.

Salt, or rather the lack of it, became less of a problem in the English fishing industry when beds of rock salt were discovered in Cheshire, in west-central England, near the end of the seventeenth century. At first the salt was mined with pick and shovel, but the development of the steam engine made it possible to pump it out. Hot water was poured down into the beds to dissolve the salt and the resulting brine was pumped to the surface. The brine was evaporated, and a fine-grained product crystallized out. The production of the English beds, however, was not enough to meet the needs of the fishing industry and furthermore the fine-grained product was not considered the best for preserving cod. Fine-grained salt causes excessive drying, or "salt burn," of the flesh, and the English product also contained calcium and magnesium, which caused the proteins in the cod flesh to coagulate and left a bitter, unpleasant taste. The coarse grains produced by solar evaporation were preferred. The Dutch developed a way to dissolve fine salt in sea water and evaporate the resulting brine in the heat of the sun to produce coarse salt with less of the objectionable calcium and magnesium. The method was introduced into England at the beginning of the eighteenth century.

The manufacture of salt in Britain provided a lucrative source of tax revenue but had an adverse social effect. The imposition of a salt tax in Scotland in 1712 produced a condition of servitude for crofters in the Highlands and the Shetland Islands who tilled small parcels of land rented from the owners. Many of the crofters also fished for part of their food. When the tax was imposed, the landowners required the crofters to supply them with cod for curing as a condition of living on the land they tilled; previously the landlords had bought the fish from fishermen. The landlords not only acted as dealers but supplied the lines, hooks, and boats, so that few or no cash transactions took place.

The crofter-fish-curing combination proved so profitable that by the 1830's large fish-curing companies replaced the landlords and established a completely monopolistic grip on the Shetland Islands by taking over the village store and keeping the crofters in perpetual indebtedness. The situation soon became intolerable, and in 1871 the Truck

Act Commission was established by the government to investigate the situation. One witness at the Commission hearing in Edinburgh reported, "The crews for the boats are hired in December or January at the same time boys are engaged as beach boys. The boy is allowed to draw his coat [charged in the company store against his anticipated wages] to go to church with, and by the time the fishing is over the boy has overdrawn his account, and is thirled [bound or contracted] to be engaged for the next season, and he is thus thirled or trucked away until he is thirled into the grave." The bitter memory of this prolonged period of exploitation of the crofters by first the landlords and then the large fish-curing companies is still very much alive in the Shetland Islands today.

Although salted dried cod supplied the European markets with fish the year around for centuries, there was also a good demand for fresh cod when it could be obtained. The best supply, of course, was in the coastal cities and fishing villages. Since there was no ice the fishermen brought the cod and other fishes to the dock alive in well-boats. There the fish were transferred to "trunks," partially submerged boxes through which the water circulated to keep the fish alive.

The practice of keeping the fish alive in the boat developed during the Middle Ages. A pool of water was accumulated in the bottom of the boat and the fish were put into this as soon as they were caught. In the seventeenth century, regular well-boats were built which were specially constructed with two water-tight bulkheads athwartship, from keel to deck, to form the well. The sides of the ship were perforated with large holes bored below the waterline to allow for a good circulation of sea water.

Well-boats with a load of live cod for the London market would proceed up the Thames estuary as far as Gravesend, at the mouth of the river, where the fish were transferred into smaller hatch-boats. The hatch-boats could be rowed farther up river to the Billingsgate fish market in London in one tide. When the market price or demand was low, the fishermen would wait at Gravesend with the live fish aboard the boats. During the summer, hatch-boats went as far as North Foreland—fifty miles east of Gravesend—to collect the fish, taking fifty to sixty bushels at a time. This method of transporting the fish alive in water was a far more reliable method than carting dead fish overland in vans during the hot weather. Toward the end of the nineteenth century, however, the fishermen could not keep the cod alive in the hatch-boats and trunks because the water in the Thames was so grossly polluted.

The well-boat fishery continued to expand in England, and by 1800 the men were fishing with long lines on Dogger Bank about 100 miles east of northern England and almost 200 miles from Gravesend. In the long-line fishery, any cod that were dead when they were hauled aboard were immediately cleaned, split, and salted on board. To bait the hooks on the long lines, each vessel took about forty-five "wash" (a wash was a unit of measure equal to about forty-three pints) of whelks, snail-like shellfish that are tough and not easily washed off the hooks. Gorges attached to the lines near the hooks prevented the cod from swallowing the hooks. As soon as a fish was landed and taken off the hook, the fishermen punctured its air bladder, which was usually inflated from the expansion of the gasses as the fish were hauled from the depths. The live fish were then placed in the well, where a cod caught in moderate depths (about thirty-fathoms or less) could normally survive for one or two weeks.

The trade in live cod, with the use of well-boats and fish chests at the dock, gave rise to a specialized group of men called "cod bangers." It was believed that the cod flesh was firmer and kept better before it finally reached the consumer if the fish was killed as soon as it was taken from the fish chests at the dock instead of dying a slow death from suffocation. Thus the practice developed of taking the live fish one at a time by the head and tail and tossing them onto the pier where the cod banger stunned them by hitting them on the snout with a short billy club. Later, because the trade was centered about the port of Grimsby on Britain's east coast, Grimsby men were colloquially called cod bangers.

Although live cod are still brought to market today—the open-air fish market in Bergen, Norway, displays cod and flounders alive in water-filled tanks for customers' selection—the usual practice is to dress and ice the fish at sea. Ice was first used to preserve cod early in the nineteenth century. Sometimes the ice was brought by sailing ships from Norway or even from the United States. During the early 1800's ice from Wenham Lake, about ten miles west of Gloucester, Massachusetts, was taken to Great Britain to supply her fishing fleets. It soon became apparent that the industry could not afford the long journey across the Atlantic with a cargo of ice, and the British abandoned Wenham Lake in favor of ice from Norway's Lake Oppegaard. However, in a move that is easily understood in the business world of the twentieth century, the Norwegian lake was renamed Wenham Lake to retain the trade name of the ice.

Some ice for the fishing fleets was cut in Britain, but because British winters are not very cold, it did not develop into more than a very local industry. Men, women, and children cut the ice, and as many as 3,000 were kept busy when the lakes and ponds were frozen deep enough.

The use of ice to preserve the catch aboard the vessels made it possible for the industry to develop and refine the beam trawl and later the otter trawl. Trawl nets caught large quantities of fish more efficiently and faster than the older hooks and lines, but fish in the large trawl catches were usually dead when they landed on deck, and thus trawl-caught fish had to be iced or salted on board. The increased catches of iced (hence, fresh) cod and other fishes brought the price of fish down to the point where it became an inexpensive everyday food item.

As with new developments in many industries, the practice of icing fish at sea was received with less than enthusiasm by the fisherman on the deck. He had grown used to the short trips of the well-boat and the live-fish trade and did not like the idea of remaining at sea for several weeks in order to load the hold with iced fish. It was the deckies' firm and loudly expressed opinion that the use of ice meant that "the owners were going to usurp our rights, tyrannize us, and keep us at sea!"

Nor was icing fish at sea the only complaint of the fishermen. "Fleeting" was introduced by the vessel owners, which—it seemed to the fishermen—was the devil's own invention to make them spend most of their lives at sea away from family, home, and hearth. In fleeting, the fishing smacks remained at sea for up to eight weeks, during which time their fish was periodically off-loaded at sea to carriers that serviced a fleet of smacks. The carriers made frequent trips to port to discharge the cargo of iced fish and returned to the fleet to make another round. Sometimes the smacks took out only enough food and water for six weeks and supplies for the remaining time were carried to them by the carriers. At the end of the eight weeks, the smacks returned to port for about a week for refit and to allow the men time to spend at home.

The fishermen hated fleeting, because in addition to the normal hazards of fishing from their small sailing ships they faced the very hazardous daily practice of transferring the catch from the smacks to the carriers in small rowing boats. The boats frequently swamped, dumping the men and the load of fish into the icy sea. And a man might easily lose a hand or arm between the pitching, bobbing boats during the off-loading operation. It was imperative to get the fish on ice aboard the carrier as quickly as possible, and the crews could not wait for calm seas to make the transfer. If the weather was bad and the seas too rough, the smacksmen dumped the catch overboard, since they carried no ice and the fish spoiled quickly on the little vessels, especially in warm weather. The potential loss of their catch and the subsequent loss of pay forced the fishermen to risk the dangers in marginal weather.

In the eyes of the vessel owners visits to the boats by "copers" from Holland was another unfortunate by-product of fleeting. Coper is an English word for one who bargains, and is derived from the Dutch word *koopen*, meaning to buy or bargain. The copers sold rum, gin, and cheap, duty-free tobacco to the fishermen, who were only too happy to barter what they had for these items to help relieve the drudgery of life aboard the smacks. The owners, however, wanted the men to fish, not spend their time getting drunk or smoking. A Royal Navy Mission to Deep Sea Fishermen was founded in the 1880's in an attempt to divert the men away from the twin evils of drink and smoke, and in 1893 an international convention was signed to forbid the activities of the copers.

The fishermen survived many changes in their ancient trade, including the change from hook-and-line fishing to trawling, the change from salt fishing to the use of ice, and the introduction of fleeting. At the turn of the century another change was made that was more revolutionary than all the others; the use of steam vessels, which meant that fishermen were no longer dependent on the vagaries of the wind— too much, too little, or from the wrong direction—to carry on their work. They were also able to make faster trips to the fishing grounds, fish the trawls with much greater efficiency, and return to port rapidly with the fish.

Although the first successful steamers had been used in the Clyde in 1812, it wasn't until fifty years later that steam engines were installed in fishing vessels. The engines were first used only to propel the vessels and were not used to lighten the labor of hauling the nets until about 1876, when the steam capstan and winch came into use. The use of steam trawlers made it possible for fish in the market to be more abundant and cheaper than they had ever been before, and made fishing profitable enough to risk long voyages to Iceland and Newfoundland and even to the New World fisheries where cod were so much more abundant than in the long-fished European seas.

The changes in the ships and the manner of fishing brought changes as well in the men who skippered the ships and served as the crews. The steam trawlermen considered themselves the vanguard of the future, pioneers in new ships using new techniques. The dory fishermen, however, looked on the trawlermen with disdain and contempt. There was something lacking, they sneered, in a man who fished from the deck of the floating iron machines rather than enduring the more arduous and risky life in an open dory. Captain Angus Walters, skipper of the famed Canadian dory schooner *Bluenose*, summed it up in a terse statement: "They're softies," he said some years ago, "not the same kind of young-uns that sailed in the schooners when I started forty years ago!"

Although skippers and crews today still face the same vagaries of fish populations and the same unknowns of weather, they do have some added advantages—radar, ship-to-shore radio, and electronic fish finders. They still recognize, however, that the ocean they work in is "a sea to be respected," in the words of one young Scottish skipper, Joseph Hey, owner and skipper of the fifty-foot *Golden Eagle*.

Joseph Hey is thirty-three years old, and as owner and skipper earns about $6,700 annually. On an average, each member of his crew earns about $2,500 a year, which doesn't approach that of men on big trawlers that fish off Norway, Iceland, and Newfoundland, but Hey and his crew feel that they have other benefits that make up for the pay. They are at home more often, there is more of a sense of close comradeship aboard their small boat, and they are dealing directly with the boat owner rather than through some impersonal agent for the owner many miles away.

Hey fishes for a variety of species throughout the year. In the summer he might go out for five days to fish for cod, hake, whiting, and other groundfish—"whatever we find," he says. The crew numbers five, including the skipper's father, and they eat and sleep up forward in the fo'c'sle.

Life on the small trawler is pretty grim, according to Hey. "We have two hauls each night which means we can get about two hours rest at a time, but I haven't got used to sleeping in a boat yet. If we go out on Monday, it's Wednesday before I can sleep. At the beginning of the week, a lot of us get seasick. . . . And we don't wash much because we need the water."

But the men of the *Golden Eagle* wouldn't give up their way of life for that of the men who work aboard the middle- and distant-water trawlers. For one thing, trawlermen have twice as many accidents as miners and twenty times as many accidents as workers in industry. Joseph Hey sums it up: "I wouldn't be a trawlerman for anything. They have a hard life."

But there is at least one trawlerman who is happiest when he is at sea, although he will be the first to agree that it is a hard life. He is George John Duncan Thompson Whur, skipper of the British distant-water trawler *Ross Orion*. He has been called one of the highest-paid fishermen in Britain; in a good year he can earn $28,000. His vessel is a four-year-old steel diesel trawler with all the modern electronics equipment available. None of this is of any help, says the skipper, if he is not in the same place as the fish, and finding them is still the hardest part of the job. Once the fish are found the numbing, bone-wearying toil begins. The big trawl is set and hauled every three hours, spilling its catch of cod or haddock onto the wet, exposed deck of the ship. "During the fishing period," says Whur, "we can work eighteen hours in twenty-four, bringing up the fish, dressing it on deck, and putting it down on ice in the pens. You get so tired you can't pick up your knife and fork when it's time to eat."

Bad weather is not the least of the skipper's worries. He is responsible for a crew of nineteen men, and although they don't talk much about the danger, they are always aware of it. A sudden winter storm out of the Arctic when they are fishing off Iceland can quickly turn the ship into an unmaneuverable, top-heavy mass of ice; the spray picked up by a howling gale quickly freezes on the rigging, masts, and superstructure in the bitter cold. It may form a crystal coat a half foot to a foot thick, adding many tons to the exposed part of the ship above the waterline. Men are sent aloft to bash away at the ice with axes or great wooden mallets. On some ships in the Arctic fishery, special hot-water and steam hoses are played on the ice to free the vessels from their massive, icy shrouds. Should these measures fail, the ship may suddenly turn-turtle, drowning all hands in the near-freezing sea. Even if a man could jump free of the capsizing vessel, he would survive only five or ten minutes in the water, which, at a temperature of about 30 to 35 degrees Fahrenheit, acts like a blotter, quickly soaking and absorbing the vital body heat. Numbness and unconsciousness quickly follow, and the doomed man silently slips into the green depths of the icy sea.

In some years, when the winter storm track and weather cycle combine to bring especially harsh conditions to the sub-Arctic fishing grounds, the specter of icing up strikes again and again at the fleets. January 1968 was such a time for the British trawlermen, with disaster touching the fishing fleet in the traditional group of three. Three trawlers out of Hull were lost in the northern seas within a two-week period that month. The first was the *St. Romanus*, 600 tons, missing since January 13 off Norway and presumed lost with a crew of twenty. The next was the *Kingston Peridot*, 658 tons, missing since January 27 off Iceland and presumed lost with her crew of twenty. The third was the *Ross Cleveland*, 600 tons, which went down with nineteen men off Iceland in what was called the worst Arctic storm in many years. Twelve of the nineteen crewmen were married and most had children at home.

Two days after the *Ross Cleveland* went down an eyewitness to the sinking miraculously appeared floating in a covered rubber life raft—trawlerman Harry Eddom, twenty-six years old, a crew member aboard the *Ross Cleveland* on its fatal trip on the Iceland fishing grounds. While the storm raged, the ship dodged into the wind and waves, barely maintaining speed and headway. As the ship iced up the officer on watch noticed that the radar scanner was held fast by the ice, and without radar the vessel could not keep track of the other trawlers around her. Harry, standing a wheel-watch in the pilot house, was probably—like most fishermen under similar circumstances—smoking a cigarette and "yarning" about other ships and other storms. When it became obvious that the scanner had to be freed, Harry was chosen to take care of it.

He was wise to the ways of the ship in a storm and remembered the ancient rule of the men at sea—"one hand for the ship and one hand for me." He put on his warmest sweater, trousers, and a woolen cap, and, over it all, a survival suit, a sort of rubber cover-all designed to conserve body heat if the wearer goes into the water. The bulky clothing and suit made walking difficult but Harry clambered up the slippery ladder to chop at the ice around the scanner. And then it happened!

The ship "just took a huge sea and wouldn't bring her head back into the wind," Harry said later in an interview. Now broadside to the wind and waves, the huge vessel heeled over and, top-heavy with ice, turned turtle. Rubber life rafts were automatically released by the contact with the water and they bobbed on the tossing waves as the CO_2 tanks did their jobs and filled the flotation compartments of the rafts. But there was no one alive to use the rafts except for Harry Eddom in his exposure suit.

Rubber life rafts are really floating igloos with an encircling roof that gives complete protection from the wind and water to anyone inside. Harry Eddom survived thirty-six hours in the raft in temperatures that hovered around the freezing mark. Doctors who attended him in the hospital after his rescue said they had never known anyone to survive such conditions for so long a period. The head of the Human Physiology Laboratory of the British Medical Research Council, Dr. Otto Edholm, interviewed Harry to obtain information which might lead to improved survival techniques for the crews of vessels which founder in Arctic waters.

Confronted by the omnipresent prospect of disaster and death at sea, it is no wonder that the European fisherman has evolved as rich a fund of superstitions as has his American counterpart. Skipper George Whur of the *Ross Orion* explains simply, "I'm a bit superstitious about a lot of things. We'll not have a woman on board ship, for instance. And we'll not say 'rabbits' on a trawler—terrible bad luck, that."

Other superstitions cover a whole spectrum of things and events. For example, it is bad luck for the crew to know how much fish they have caught; only the captain, the first mate, and the owners ashore should know the amount of the catch stored on ice in the hold. If a ship sails on a Friday, the crew is sure to drown at sea. To sail on a Sunday is to invoke the wrath of God, and to speak of a minister while the ship is at sea is considered sacrilegious. Fishermen can talk with impunity about any of the creatures in the sea, but to talk of a salmon is to sink the ship. It is also considered extremely risky and a certain invitation to bad luck to talk about a corpse or to mention the word "chicken."

In addition to his adherence to the list of superstitious dos and don'ts, many of the fishermen, especially the old-timers, refused to ac-

[77]

cept modern inventions to help them in their ancient trade. They'd rather ignore the fish finders, sonars, and scientifically calculated charts of fish distribution in favor of what some old salt told them in a pub. Gordon Eddie, Technical Director of the British White Fish Authority, said in an interview in *World Fishing* magazine that too many trawler skippers relied on a mass of vague, conflicting, inaccurate, and sometimes deliberately misleading information to find a good school of cod. And all too often, he added, they rely too much on "grandfather's little black book."

The skippers were quick to reply to Mr. Eddie's critical remarks. Said one, "We are always getting office workers telling us how to catch fish!" Another skipper asked the rhetorical question, "Does Mr. Eddie believe that codfish go 'round with a calendar around their necks? Cod gather at little spots at the same time each year, most years, but there are times when, for some reason, they do not. That's when 'grandfather's little black book' can tell us where he caught fish under the same sort of situation, maybe before we were born. That can mean the difference between a good trip of fish, and nothing. A man can have aboard all the scientific equipment you like but it won't trace fish that are fifty miles away. You've got to out-guess the fish; a machine won't do it for you."

Skippers Whur and Hey and trawlerman Eddom are typical of the men of the Western nations who fish for cod and other fish in the North Atlantic. They are also very much like the fishermen from behind the Iron Curtain. The life and working conditions of Polish trawlermen were detailed in a study, "Psychosociological Problems of Work in the Fisherman's Occupation," by Aurelia Polańska, published in *Prace Morskiego Instytutu Rybackiego*, a Polish journal of the Sea Fisheries Institute in Gdynia. It has been translated into English.

The vessels in which the Polish fisherman sails, the nets he sets and hauls, and the fish he dresses are the same as the ones his Western counterpart encounters. A fisherman from a Polish or Soviet trawler could trade places with a fisherman from a British or French or American trawler and both could immediately fall to work with barely a break in routine. Not only are the ships and gear the same, the drudgery, boredom, and danger at sea and the seemingly aimless way they live during their brief breaks ashore are very much the same.

The report states that although the Polish fisherman's pay is above that country's national average, the men work an average of eighteen hours per day, making the hourly rate very low. Many of the men find life at sea aboard a trawler dull, monotonous, and, to some, degrading. The cold, damp conditions on the ship are a hardship over which they have little control, and they complain about the sameness of the surroundings—the cabins, the mess facilities, the sea itself. The work is hard and, at times, dangerous, and the hours are long with little time at home with their wives and children. The little spare time the Polish fishermen have while at sea is spent largely in making up for lost sleep. They read a lot, listen to the radio, play chess and checkers, or just chat.

Perhaps the hardest aspect of the work for the fisherman to accept is the attitude among the "landlubbers," who are fond of quoting a derogatory old saw: "If he is stupid and strong, he's a born fisherman." And yet a Polish trawlerman knows that if he changed jobs and worked on land he would be employed as an unskilled worker, unless he was an engineer.

Some of the Polish trawlermen are proud of their occupation and look forward to the days at sea, and some feel they have a carefree life: "I give the wife the money, and as for myself, I get food and clothing free, so I've got no worries." They seem to have a great sense of personal well-being at sea, although the average fisherman is not able to explain exactly what it is about the work that appeals to him: "I feel good, I couldn't work in a factory again" . . . "When I am on land too long, I feel an urge to get back to sea" . . . "There's a sort of something that drives me to the ship."

For these men the work is varied, interesting, and rewarding. A factory hand, they say, does work that is repetitive, simple, and requires routine action. The fisherman, on the other hand, works with different gear and on various fishing grounds where the species composition of the catch varies, which makes his job less monotonous. Even the changes in weather conditions make it necessary to adjust life and work on board ship to the different seasons.

Many years before permanent settlements were established in Newfoundland and Maine, cod fishermen came ashore regularly, building stages on which to clean, dry, and salt their catches. (Bettmann Archive)

7

Cod and the Discovery of America

MEN ARE DRAWN TO NEW LANDS for a variety of reasons. Some are lured by tales of fabulous cities of gold or of diamonds scattered on stream beds like so many pebbles. Some look for freedom to worship God as they choose or for release from the crowds of populous cities. Some seek the nebulous dream of "a new life," while others flee the law to prolong their old one. But the *pescadores* who sailed to the uncharted shores of the northwest Atlantic were drawn by no visionary's dreams or idealist's goals. They sought the tangible wealth of the codfish that swarmed in the cold depths over the fishing banks of the New World.

Every schoolboy can recite the facts that give Columbus the credit for the discovery of America, but Europeans stepped on the shores of this continent long before 1492. Many of them were cod fishermen, who came to dry their salted catch on the rocky beaches of Newfoundland. The cod fishery on the Grand Bank of Newfoundland was in full swing by the end of the fifteenth century not too long after Columbus made his landfall in the Caribbean.

There is considerable dispute as to exactly who were the first explorers of northeastern America, and nationalistic claimants to the honor are legion. According to who is telling the tale, the pioneers were Scandinavian, Italian, French, Irish, or English; even the ancient Greeks are given partial credit.

The earliest explorers of the New World of whom we have certain evidence were the hardy Scandinavians called Vikings. These were hunters and farmers who made their homes in the *viks* (fjords) of Norway's rugged coast. They were not primarily fishermen, although they did hunt whales and seals, and caught cod in the cold deeps of the fjords and coastal waters. The Norsemen were open-boat fishermen, using lines and jigs made from lead, bone, and deer antlers. These were fished with horsehair and sheep-gut handlines.

As early as the sixth century, Viking fishermen in open boats had gone as far west as the Hebrides, the Shetland Islands, the Orkney Islands, and the north coast of Scotland. The Norse reached Iceland in about 850 and Greenland, discovered by Eric the Red, in 982.

Our knowledge of the activities of the Vikings in North America is derived from relics of their settlement at Epaves Bay in northern Newfoundland and from the Icelandic sagas, epic poems, and prose narratives that tell of the voyages of Eric's son, Leif the Lucky, and other Northmen to "Vinland."

Leif and his brothers, Thorvald and Thorstein, sailed from Greenland in the summer of 1001 on a long journey that took them to many parts of the northeast coast of North America. Some of the places they visited have been readily recognized by historians from the descriptions given in the sagas, others are still the subject of long arguments. One place the Norseman discovered was bleak and forbidding; in the words of the saga, "great ice mountains lay inland back from the sea, and it was as a [tableland of] flat rock all the way from the sea to the ice mountains, and the country seemed to them to be entirely devoid of good qualities." The Vikings called the place Helluland, land of rocks, probably the coast of Labrador.

Leif's flotilla of dragon ships sailed farther south and found "a level wooded land, and there were broad stretches of white sand, where they went." This they called Markland, recognized today as Newfoundland.

A third place they named Vinland because of the abundance of grape-producing vines. It was a hospitable land with good forage for the cattle, mild winters, and an abundance of fish, especially "larger salmon than they had ever seen before." Leif went back to Greenland, but his brother, Thorvald, returned to Vinland and established a settlement there, "supplying themselves with food by fishing" during the winter. Their catch may have been salmon, but more likely it was cod.

The exact location of Vinland has been debated hotly. Various sites

[82]

along the coastlines of Nova Scotia, Massachusetts, and Rhode Island have been suggested. Some even believe the Norsemen traveled as far west as Wisconsin. If Vinland was in Nova Scotia or New England, cod and salmon probably furnished the principal catch of the Viking winter fishery. Cod have been abundant throughout history in this region, and could have been caught by the Vikings with little effort. The cod is not mentioned often in the sagas, perhaps because it was so common in the Norse diet that it did not deserve discussion. It was the same during the heyday of the New England salt-bank fishery, as we have already noted—when the dorymen spoke of The Fish (you could almost hear the capitals as they said the words), they meant cod, and everyone understood. It may have been the same with the Vikings.

The Vikings did not attempt to set up any trade with dried cod from the New World, since there was not much hope of making a profit from a cargo of cod when there was cod aplenty in the home waters of Scandinavia. The sagas relate that the longboats of Leif and the later Viking explorers returned with cargoes of grape vines, grapes, timber, game, and fish.

Quarrels among the bands of Vikings, and battles with the natives of the North American continent, caused the abandonment of the settlements in Markland and Vinland. The Vikings withdrew to Greenland and Iceland, and there clung tenaciously to the rocky, chilled shores. They no longer made long journeys in their dragon ships, and for nearly 500 years the lands to the west existed only in the sagas and in sailor yarns told in the waterfront taverns of Europe.

During this time the western ocean was shrouded in a gloomy legend that called it a dead and stagnant sea inhabited by monsters, covered with masses of weed that trapped ships and men for eternity, half-hidden in fog and mist. Then, with the emerging Age of Reason, men once again looked to the western horizon. The Basques claim the honor of the rediscovery of Newfoundland early in the fourteenth century, in the course of their whaling expeditions. Basques of Cape Breton may have discovered the cod fishing around Newfoundland a century before Christopher Columbus made his first voyage, but there is no proof of this claim. The first authentic records of the Basques in Newfoundland are dated 1528, whereas documents show that Bretons and Normans fished in Newfoundland waters in 1508.

Perhaps the discoverers of the Newfoundland cod fishery were John Cabot and his son Sebastian, Italian seamen on a voyage of exploration for the English king, Henry VII. On June 24, 1497, Giovanni Caboto (anglicized to John Cabot) and a company of Englishmen planted the flag of England on a land in the New World, on Cape Breton Island.

Original documents relating to Cabot's voyage are scattered, but Dr. Edward G. Bourne, Professor of History at Yale, offers the private letters of two Italians visiting London in 1497–98 as reports of his discoveries. One letter in particular, written on December 18, 1497, makes specific mention of the abundance of fishes there: "the sea is covered with fishes, which are caught not only with the net but with baskets, a stone being tied to them in order that the baskets may sink in the water." The Englishmen on the voyage recognized the commercial possibilities of the fish in the New World. Their ships, they said, "will bring so many fishes that this kingdom will no longer have need of Iceland, from which country there comes a very great store of fish which are called stock-fish."

In 1498, Cabot and a company of Bristol merchants made a second voyage to the northeast coast of North America, including Newfoundland. They reported that the sea "yieldeth plentie of fish and those very great, as seals, . . . but specially there is a great abundance of that kinde of fish (much like unto tunnies) which the savages call baccalaos."

If the report is correct, the use of the term *baccalaos* adds another contender to the list of first-comers to America. Since *bacalao* is the Spanish word for cod, this suggests that southern Europeans had been on the American shores before Cabot landed and perhaps even before Columbus landed in the West Indies. Dr. C. P. Idyll of the Institute of Marine and Atmospheric Science in Miami states that Portuguese fishermen have a tradition that their countrymen had begun the *Campanha Bachaloeira* (the Cod Campaign, or, fishery for cod) in 1493. Thus, although there are no records to authenticate these claims, there seems to be good reason to suspect that someone from Mediterranean Europe might have visited Newfoundland before Cabot. This is further substantiated by a statement by Dr. Richard J. Houk, of the Department of Geography at De Paul University, who made a detailed study of the Portuguese fishing industry. He credits the master mariners from Portugal with dispelling some of the fears and superstitions then associated with sailing over the uncharted Atlantic Ocean. There is evidence that two Portuguese navigators not only journeyed to North

America in 1463 but that they also reported the abundance of cod on the banks off Newfoundland.

Active participation by the Portuguese in a Newfoundland banks fishery for cod was not begun until later, however. Following Cabot's 1498 voyage, vessels from Bristol began to exploit the area. The ships sailed in the spring, first to Portugal for salt. With the cargo of salt in the holds, they then sailed to Newfoundland to fish for cod, which was split and salted aboard ship. Back to Portugal they went to sell the fish and to buy cargoes of wine, olive oil, and salt. (This was an early form of the "Golden Triangle" practiced in the eighteenth century by New England vessels trading in codfish, rum, and slaves.) In 1504, French vessels arrived on the Newfoundland banks to fish for cod and were followed by the Portuguese in 1506.

The Portuguese cod fishery helped those masters of navigation to make many of their now-famous voyages of discovery to Africa, India, Brazil, Japan, and Indonesia. As in the homeland, the men aboard the ships needed a protein food that could be preserved in warm climates. The abundant supply of dried salt cod from the northwest Atlantic was essential to the success of these far-ranging expeditions.

During the sixteenth century, the European fishing fleet on the Newfoundland banks grew to meet the homeland demand for cod. There was little real effort to colonize the land. The crews built piers to tie up to and stages on which to dry the fish, but these were abandoned when the fishing season was over and the fleets returned home. It was not until about 1618 that British "planters" accompanied the fishing fleet from England to establish a permanent base on Newfoundland.

During the fishing season some of the men fished while others salted and dried the fish on the shore. At night the processing crew returned to the ship to sleep, where they felt it was safer, in an unknown country inhabited by unknown people. The shoreside accommodations were very simple. After a while, however, the men began to sleep ashore at night, and barracks and other living quarters were built.

Although the French had pioneered the Newfoundland fishery for cod, the English soon entered and began to dominate it. The English quickly developed greater markets for their salt cod. Early in the sixteenth century, Catholic Spain welcomed the British salt cod, and English fishermen were encouraged to seek additional populations to exploit. Their vessels beat along the coast, moving southward and westward, testing for new fishing banks with the sounding lead and the fishing line. Browns Bank, off the southern tip of Nova Scotia, and St. George's Bank (now simply Georges Bank), south and west of Browns, proved to be rich fishing grounds. The rough, craggy bottom of the gulf of Maine was a veritable bonanza of cod; a century or two later it was to make the fortune of many a New Englander and give rise to the Boston Codfish Aristocracy.

The discovery of one now-famous part of New England resulted from the search for a commodity completely apart from codfish but in which the cod had a featured role. On March 26, 1602, the ship *Concord*, commanded by Bartholomew Gosnold, departed Falmouth, England, headed for the shores of the New World. Gosnold had two objectives: to trade with the natives and to search for sassafras trees. Sassafras had a very practical and urgent use in Europe at that time: it was a prime ingredient in the European pharmacopaeia as a treatment for syphilis. Variously known then as "the French disease" by the Spaniards and English, "the Spanish disease" by the French, and so on, syphilis was considered a native American disease. The returning voyagers of Columbus' expeditions are accused of taking it to Europe, where it soon reached widespread, epidemic proportions. All manner of materials were tried as curative agents, and extracts of the aromatic sassafras (also a product of the New World) were among the most popular agents. Even today, folk medicine calls for a draft of sassafras tea to "purify the blood," and an extract of sassafras root is one of the flavoring substances in root beer.

Gosnold's records note that on May 14, 1602, the *Concord* reached "a mighty headland." Aboard the ship were two adventurers, John Brereton and Gabriel Archer, who wrote detailed accounts of the historical voyage. It was Archer who told of the naming of the headland: "The 15th day we had again sight of the land, which made ahead, being as we thought an island, we called it Shoal Hope. Near this cape we came to anchor in 15 fathoms, where we took great store of codfish, for which we altered the name, and called it Cape Cod."

Gosnold himself immediately recognized the commercial possibilities of the "great store of codfish." He coasted down what is now Vineyard Sound past a string of forested, jewel-like islands which today bear names like Nashawena, Nonamesset, and Cuttyhunk. He named

[86]

the group the Elizabeth Islands—the collective name that exists today—in honor of his sovereign, Elizabeth I, the Virgin Queen.

Then, as now, the Elizabeth Islands and the curved peninsula of Cape Cod supported a fair abundance of sassafras trees, and the success of Gosnold's trip was assured. But it was the codfish that provided the important entries for Gosnold's report. He noted that "in the months of March, April and May, there is upon this coast, better fishing, and in as great plentie, as in Newfoundland. . . . And, besides, the places . . . were but in seven faddome water and within less than a league of the shore; where, in New-found-land they fish in fortie or fiftie fad-dome water and farre off."

Fishermen were not far behind this voyage of discovery. As a result of Gosnold's reports on the abundance of codfish, Bristol merchants provided Martin Pring with two vessels to explore the cod resources. In 1603, Pring arrived off the coast of the strand and found that Gos-nold had not exaggerated. The land, too, he found well suited to the shoreside activities of the fishery, providing not only an abundance of cod but also an abundance of rocky ground on which to dry the prod-uct for shipment back to Europe. "Wee found," wrote Pring, "an ex-cellent fishing for cod which are better than those of New-found-land and withall we saw good and rockie ground fit to drie them upon." By 1616, vessels were regularly fishing off the New England coast. One was commanded by Captain John Smith, whose claim to fame is not codfish but a romanticized alliance with the Virginia Indian maiden, Pocahontas.

In an effort to entice settlers to the New World, Smith wrote rap-turously, "And is it not a pretty sport to pull up two pence, six pence and twelve pence as fast as you can haul and vere a line; he is a very bad fisher who can not kill in one day one, two or three hundred cod, which dressed and dried be sold for ten shillings a hundred.

"Honorable and worthy countrymen," Smith urged, "let not the meanness of the word fish distaste you, for it will afford as good gold as the Mines of Guiana or Potassie, with less hazard and charge, and more certainty and facility."

Smith's propagandizing fell on deaf ears. His fellow countrymen at home had heard other tales of the land they called New England— that it was a barren land which yielded no gold, silk, spices, or wool. Savages roamed its rocky shores and the wintry winds caused great trees to freeze to their cores and split open with a crack like a musket shot. Such a land did not even deserve the name of their beloved motherland.

Throughout the first two decades of the seventeenth century no attempts were made to establish permanent settlements on the bleak New England coast. The fishers were content to catch and dry their cod during the favorable seasons, and to abandon the waters in the winter in the face of the howling northeast storms and blinding snows for which the region is notorious. But times were changing, and when a band of persecuted Englishmen—religious malcontents, some called them—sailed from Delftshaven, Holland, in July 1620, the New England coast and its productive fishing banks were destined for permanent settlement and exploitation.

The Pilgrim Fathers thought they were heading for the Virginia colony, but autumn gales and treacherous shoals forced them to seek a more northerly landfall. It had been a long, difficult journey aboard the cramped *Mayflower*. Few of the Pilgrim band had acquired sea legs and the stormy Northwest Atlantic made life miserable for even the doughtiest of the travelers. Tempers and food and supplies were short. Furthermore, another essential commodity was running out; a manuscript prepared in 1622 explained, "For we could not now take time for further search or consideration; our victuals being much spent, especially our beer." So they landed at the earliest opportunity.

Dr. Robert G. Raymer, biographer of John Winthrop, reports that the Pilgrims resorted to fishing to help relieve the shortage of fresh food. As the *Mayflower* neared the shoals off the shores of the New World, the vessel hove to in about thirty fathoms of water and "took in less than two hours with a fish-hook sixty seven cod fish, most of them very great fish—some a yard and a half long and a yard in compass." All this, says Dr. Raymer, at about four o'clock in the morning. Later in the day, they heaved the sounding lead and found fifty fathoms of water, "and being in calm, we heaved out hooks again and took twenty six cods, so we all feasted with fish this day."

Once the Plymouth colony was established, the Pilgrims lost no time in establishing a profitable fishing industry—the first industry in the embryonic United States. And in 1623, just three years after the *Mayflower* landed, merchants from Bristol, Exeter, Dorchester, Shrewsbury, Plymouth, and other parts of western England formed an association known as the Company of Laconia to catch cod and trade with

Europe. As the settlers moved to other sections of the New England colony's coast, they continued to exploit the abundant cod resource. The cool, relatively dry winter season was just right for making stockfish, and this led to the development of a winter fishery in New England. While the land was rocky and gave up a meager crop of farm produce, the sea was rich and productive, yielding its crop with relatively little effort.

The profits to be made from harvesting the sea attracted more settlers, and it is an open question as to which was the more important factor in the colonization of New England: the cod or the quest for religious freedom. The English fishery scientist and historian C. L. Cutting states, "The sole purpose of the first settlers in New Hampshire was not to escape from religious persecution but to acquire wealth by fishing and trading." And Walter Muir Whitehill, Director and Librarian of the Boston Athenaeum, relates an incident, perhaps apocryphal, in which a Marblehead, Massachusetts, fisherman squelches a preacher. "Our ancestors came not here for religion," said the old salt. "Their main end was to catch fish." An anonymous writer of New England history said it in a somewhat more gracious manner when he wrote that the first settlers of New England arrived there to "serve their God and to Fish." Dr. Harold A. Innis, the Canadian chronicler of the North American cod fisheries, agrees that the possibilities of developing a fishing industry had a part in attracting the Pilgrims to Plymouth.

Whatever the reasons for the settlement of the New England colonies, fishing became a very important occupation of the settlers soon after their arrival. Although the Pilgrims of Plymouth and the Puritans of the Massachusetts Bay colony at first did not consider the idea of founding maritime communities, they wound up by catching fish. There are persistent tales that cod caught in Massachusetts Bay waters saved some of the pioneers from starvation in those early and lean years. As time passed, fishing by New Englanders changed from an emergency measure to a fast-growing industry. England and continental Europe represented a rich market where the dried cod could be exchanged for manufactured goods. Thus it was that as early as 1634, a Marblehead merchant prince floated a fishing fleet of eight vessels to prosecute the trade.

Governor John Winthrop proudly noted that just one generation after the Massachusetts Bay colony was established as a tiny beachhead on the raw hostile shore, 300,000 dried cod were shipped to market. In his journal for June 2, 1641, Winthrop wrote, "These straits set our people on work to provide fish, clapboards, plank, etc. and to sow hemp and flax (which prospered very well) and to look out to the West Indies for a trade for cotton." He knew that New England depended on the outside world in its new economy, and his spirit was lifted every time another ship splashed off the ways at Boston to carry New England salt codfish to markets where "idolotrous Roman Catholics paid good money for them."

The Pilgrims eagerly set themselves to the task of becoming fishermen. In the productive New England waters, said one, "thou may'st reap without sowing—yet not without God's blessing; 'twas the Apostles' calling." The industrious New Englanders took to the ocean fishery as if they had been born to it. Fishing settlements became fishing villages, then fishing towns, and finally, as we know them even today, fishing cities. The names of the hamlets the fishermen hailed from then are names still familiar to any school boy of the twentieth century—Marblehead, Salem, Boston, and Gloucester.

Marblehead early sent her sons to sea questing for cod. In 1731, there were between 5,000 and 6,000 fishermen in Massachusetts alone, and of 400 vessels from the Bay State, 160 of them sailed out of Marblehead. Gloucester also figured prominently as a center of the industry. John J. Babson, who wrote a history of the town of Gloucester in 1860, noted that in 1624 no less than fifty vessels from Gloucester fished with handlines in the offing of Maine and Massachusetts. The grounds used in those early days are still fished by trawlermen today, and include Jeffreys Ledge, Cashes Ledge, and Nantucket Shoals. Some of the places were named by fishermen to commemorate a shipmate or some nautical event; thus we can read names on modern charts such as Toothaker Ridge, Fippennies (Five Pennies?) Ledge, Sharer Ridge, and Three Dory Ridge.

It was not long before the scope of the New Englander's operations changed and expanded. As early as 1708 New England vessels had ventured to the Nova Scotian banks, and in 1748 the first catch of cod was landed from Georges Bank 150 miles east of Boston. Some fishermen were pushing even farther away. In 1757, Gloucester vessels sailed to the Grand Bank off Newfoundland, where they joined vessels from England, France, Spain, and Portugal in seeking the cod so abundant on the productive bank. The fishing was so much more successful there than on the New England banks that by 1788 as many as sixty Gloucester vessels were fishing on Grand Bank. Presumably fishermen went to distant grounds instead of fishing the local waters because cod became scarce locally in the late eighteenth century. Few fishermen would risk a long trip offshore in small wooden vessels if cod were abundant nearby.

But cod were abundant on the offshore banks and the fisheries— and the men who owned the ships—prospered. The fisher-barons of the time were not in the least ashamed to acknowledge the source of their wealth. Benjamin Pickman of Salem built himself a fine house in 1750, and advertised the industry that provided his prosperity by placing half models of codfish on every stair end in the front hall of his house. Pickman's house no longer exists, but according to Walter Muir Whitehill one of the wooden cod half models is preserved in the Peabody Museum in Salem.

The New England cod fishery served the early settlers well because it gave them work to do in the winter. New England summers are short, and when the farmer's crops were in and winter's frost locked the soil, there was precious little source of income. Farmers inland from the coast marched off to work in the virgin forests of white pine, fir, spruce, and maple that cloaked the nearby hills. Here they began the lumbering industry that was to follow the growth of the virgin timber across the country to the Pacific shore.

Farmers near the coast, however, took to the seas for their winter livelihood. The sea provided profitable employment, furnishing an important supply of food and an excellent medium of exchange. The dried salt cod that was draped across every available rock or on specially built wooden racks, or flakes, meant money in the pocket of the farmers near the coast. C. L. Woodbury, a nineteenth-century historical-economist, summed it up in his book *The Relation of the Fisheries to the Discovery and Settlement of North America*, in 1880:

> It [the cod fishery] thus also gave to the industrious the great boon of independence, the foundation of character in the individual, and in the State. . . . The continuous employment a residence on these coasts afforded to the fisherman, gave him great advantages over the European and those who had no winter fishery at their doors, and the fishing population rapidly increased in numbers and prosperity, bringing with it commerce and an agri-

cultural population. Let me be clear, neither Pilgrims nor Puritans were its pioneers; neither the axe, the plough, nor the hoe led it to these shores; neither the devices of the chartered companies nor the commands of royalty. It was the discovery of the winter fishery on its shores that led New England to civilization, and fed alike the churchmen and the strange emigrants who came with the romance of their faith in their hearts, and the *lex talionis* [law of retaliation] in their souls to persecute because they had been persecuted.

8

Codfish, Rum, and Slaves

BESIDES CATCHING COD TO EAT themselves and to sell to
Europe, the New Englanders soon found another market for their harvest from the sea. The growth of slavery on the tobacco plantations in
Virginia and the sugar plantations on the Caribbean islands provided
steady demand for cod as food for the slaves. The best, "merchantable" grades of fish, went to Europe and the worst, or "refuse" grades,
went for the slaves. Meanwhile, the same ships that took cod to Europe
were used to transport Africans back to the New World as slaves. The
cod was thus one of the essential props in a three-cornered trade that is
often called "The Golden Triangle."

The triangle was simplicity itself. A New England vessel (they were
not yet American) sailed from Boston, Salem, or Marblehead with a
cargo of salt cod bound for ports in Portugal or Spain. After the fish
was sold, the vessel then proceeded to the Guinean coast of West Africa where the captain bought slaves. Next the vessel with its black
cargo sailed on the "Middle Passage" to the West Indies to sell the
slaves and take on a cargo of sugar and molasses for the rum distilleries
in Newport and Boston. A variation of the triangle carried the rum to
Guinea to be exchanged for slaves, and codfish to the West Indies to
be used as slave food and exchanged for the sugar and rum.

The Golden Triangle was short-lived; it flourished only for about a
half century and declined during the years of the American Revolution. While it lasted, however, it brought unimaginable misery to the

slaves, profit to the ship owners, and wealth to some families whose names read like a modern-day directory of New England's "400."

Slavery, of course, did not arise with the development of the plantation system in the southern colonies nor with the development of the rum trade in the New England colonies. Slavery was simply the method by which abundant cheap labor was obtained for whatever menial work there was to do. The practice of slavery among men is an ancient one, and the status of a slave varied tremendously from one culture to the next. Almost all slaves were captured as prizes of war.

Africa bore the brunt of much of this exploitation of one man by another. From ancient times into the twentieth century, the plunder of war and the plunder of outright exploitation of the African continent included gold, ivory, and Negro slaves. Many Africans owned Negro slaves and many sold them to Moslems, who sold them in turn to traders in Arabia and Persia. European exploitation of the Africans, however, probably was the most rigorously conducted enterprise. And the New Englanders made it more so. By the seventeenth century, a Negro slave was bought in Africa for $25 (or the equivalent in rum or other trade goods) and sold in America for $150. (It was not until early in the nineteenth century that slaves were being sold for ten or twenty times that much in the South, these Negroes usually being well trained, not "raw merchandise" fresh from the barracoons of the Guinea coast.)

A preview of the New England triangular trade was the voyage of the sixteenth-century British slaver Sir John Hawkins. He had taken a cargo of slaves from Africa and sold them in what is now Colombia, South America, and set sail on May 31, 1565, for the return trip to England. Contrary winds delayed his return passage along the welling Gulf Stream, and soon the food supply aboard ship diminished. On August 23, they were on the Grand Bank off Newfoundland in 130 fathoms of water. "Wee caught a greate many cod here which relieved our sore distress," he noted in his journal. With salt cod in the hold for food and for sale when they reached England, the vessel beat to the eastward. Safe once again in England, they gave thanks to God for their arrival in safety "with the losse of 20 persons in all the voyage, and profitable to the venturers of the said voyage."

The Pilgrim Fathers had not been too long in the New World when they too began to cast about for avenues of trade, sniffing out any opportunity for lucrative commerce. John Winthrop, wrote in his *Jour-*

nal on February 26, 1638, "Mr. Peirce, in the Salem ship, the *Desire*, returned from the West Indies after seven months. He had been at Providence [island in the Caribbean] and brought some cotton, and tobacco, and negroes, etc., from thence, and salt from Tertugos. Dry fish and strong liquors are the only commodities for those parts."

Later, the merchants discovered they could add another valuable commodity to the return cargo. The salt needed to cure the cod could be had from the solar salt works of the Indies. In correspondence between "merchant adventurers" one wrote, "The ships that shall bring Moores may come home laden with salt which may beare most of the chardge, if not all of it."

The real beginning of the New England salt cod-rum-slave trade, however, is credited to the voyage of the Boston vessel *Rainbowe* in 1645. Under the command of a Captain Smith, she took on a cargo of salt cod and barrel staves and departed Boston bound for Madeira, the Portuguese islands off the northwest coast of Africa. The salt cod found a ready and eager market there and no doubt the New World barrel staves were quickly bought as well.

Captain Smith left Madeira and sailed to the south and east for the Guinea coast. In the barracoons of the slave traders, Captain Smith hoped to invest the gold he had received for his salt cod and staves and gain a profit with some of the easy money he heard the slavers were making. When he arrived, however, he found few slaves for sale and had to bide his time, probably impatiently, in the harbor. He wanted at least a modest cargo of slaves but knew he must respect the business "ethics" of the flourishing slave trade.

The ethics required that buyers such as Captain Smith purchase slaves only from dealers. Many dealers were Arabs but most were Negroes who sold their fellow countrymen and—if the dealers drank too much rum celebrating a sale—sometimes woke up as slaves themselves aboard a ship many miles at sea. The dealers often captured villagers by raiding their tiny settlements many miles inland. But slaves most often were sold to dealers by victorious chiefs at the end of an intertribal war. The luckless captives were marched to the sea in a kaffle, a procession in which each slave marched in single file, yoked to his or her neighbors in front and back with a wooden or iron collar. At the harborside trading settlement, the slaves remained confined in compounds until hundreds were gathered to provide a good supply for the buyers.

Although buyers did not themselves go out and capture Negroes for slaves, the impatient Captain Smith could wait no longer. A slave ship out of London also lay at anchor in the harbor, and the Yankees and Britishers concocted a scheme to have a little diversion and at the same time, they hoped, get the black cargo needed to start home with.

The Africans ashore soon were startled by the sound of shouts, curses, and small-arms fire from the two vessels in the harbor. Apparently a fight had broken out between the two, and the *Rainbowe* and the British ship were exchanging shots. The Africans gathered on the shore to watch when, without warning, one of the ships fired a small cannon into the village and the watching crowd. Many of the horrified watchers were killed or wounded and in the confusion landing parties from the vessels captured a few dazed onlookers. The captains divided the captives but the *Rainbowe* received just two Negroes as her share. The stratagem had not been very successful after all. Nevertheless, when Captain Smith sailed westward to New England with his slaves aboard, he blazed the trail for the hundreds of slave ships to follow.

To the New Englanders, the slave trade was simply another facet of their seaborne industry that included fishing, whaling, and the transport of food and other goods. Less than a century after the Pilgrims landed, Massachusetts alone had more than 600 ships going offshore, half of them engaged in foreign trade with the West Indies and Europe. Alan Villiers remarks that the New England fisheries had become so valuable that a quarter of a million quintals of dried salt fish (almost all of it cod) was exported annually to Spain, Portugal, and other European nations. With the extension of their commerce into the slave trade, the sugar trade, and the rum trade, the Yankees brought into full flower the lucrative Golden Triangle.

The New England vessels, built from local timber, carried surplus food and whatever manufactured products were available. The cargoes included salt cod, beans, peas, hay, barrel staves, horses, lumber, and miscellaneous goods. As a result of their diligence in trade, the shrewd Yankees (their business opponents called them conniving) made New England the greatest slave-trading section of eighteenth-century America.

The slave trade was founded on the economic interdependence of New England, Africa, and the Caribbean islands. The islands, although producing great amounts of sugar, needed the food items to feed the slaves that worked the cane fields and sugar mills. And they needed the lumber and manufactured products of New England, which in turn was dependent upon the West Indies for the sugar and molasses. The third partner in the triangle, Africa, was eager for the New England rum, cloth, trinkets, and bar iron for which the slaves, sorely needed as cheap labor in the Caribbean islands and plantation colonies, were exchanged.

The ship owners and their captains worked the profitable multifaceted trade system with as many variations as could be devised. And the ship owners, mindful only of their profit, provided detailed, *written* instructions for the captains, frequently leaving little to the initiative and imagination of the seafarers. The excerpts below, from a letter from Samuel Waldo to Captain Samuel Rhodes, blueprint a course of action that is a far cry from the haphazard adventure of Captain Smith and the *Rainbowe*.

Boston, March 12th, 1734

Sir, With my Sloop *Affrica* which you command I desire you'll make all possible dispatch for Barbadoes where I have recommended You to my Friend Mr. James Pemberton who will I hope be capable of serving you in disposall of Some considerable part of your Cargo att a good rate and giveing You as much Cash for the same as the amount or near it. . . .

What of your Cargo You may not have Opportunity of selling att Barbadoes att a good rate (so for Cash), You may probably dispose of att some one or more of the Leward Islands takeing either money or Rum in Pay which done you are to proceed for the Island of St. Eustatious. . . .

You'll also with full Produce of the West Indies Cargo you have now aboard Invest in a Cargo of Rum for Guinea, I compute my Effects will be near extensive enough to load your Sloop with Rum. . . .

You'll with all possible Expedition go for Guinea, there Trade in such manner and places as You think best. You will be a judge of what may be most for my Intrist, so I shall intirely confide that You'll act accordingly in the Purchase of Negros, Gold Dust or any other the produce of that Country with which You'll as soon as possible make your Return to me either by way of the West Indies or Virginia shore You'll sell Your Slaves either for Gold Silver or good Bills of Exch'e. . . .

If in your Return hither from Virginia You think well of taking a moderate Loading of wheat You'll do it as from the West
Indies You'll endeavour the bringing a Cargo of Molasses or anything else You may think will do better. . . .

The records do not show the results of Captain Rhodes's voyage,
but there is little doubt that it was successful and that he made a profit
for the owner of the vessel and probably a bonus for himself. The fortunes of the trade were usually stacked in favor of the New England
traders. And if the odds were not favorable, they were made so.

The trade goods delivered to Africa were the poorest grade—the
cloth was inferior quality and so was the rum. One Rhode Island merchant, in his instructions to the captain of a slaver, wrote, "In Guinea,
make yr Chief Trade with the blacks. [They were easier to cheat.]
Worter yr rum as much as possible and sell as much by the short measure as you can."

Some of the sharpest conniving, however, was in the quality of the
salt cod delivered to the West Indies as food for the slaves on the sugar
plantations. It provided an outlet for the New Englander's "rejects"
and a way for the plantation manager to obtain a cheap supply of protein to keep his charges alive and productive.

The condition for slaves aboard a New England slaver varied from
poor to unbelievably horrible. The only solid food the slave ships
could carry had to be salted, pickled, or dried. Liquids included water,
of course, and beer and wine for the ship's officers (the rum was for
trade only). Since the slavers carried a minimum crew, food for the or-
dinary seaman was no problem. His normal fare was salt meat, beans,
and salt cod, and there usually was enough water aboard to freshen the
salt foods and soak the dried ones. But when the vessel made the voyage across the Middle Passage with a cargo of slaves (some vessels carried as many as 600), water was strictly rationed. Precious little was
available for drinking, and cooked food was limited to beans or rice in
which the water absorbed by the food is made available to the eater.

There were exceptions; an occasional vessel carried plenty of water
and few slaves on the Middle Passage, in which case salt meat and salt
cod appeared in the slave diet. A crewman on one such slaver reported, "Our slaves had two meals a day, one in the morning consist-
ing of boiled yams and the other in the afternoon of boiled horse-beans
and slabber sauce poured over each. This sauce was made of chunks of

old Irish beef and rotten salt fish stewed to rags and well seasoned with cayenne pepper. The negroes were so fond of it that they would pick out the little bits and share them out; but they didn't like the horse-beans."

There were two schools of thought among the captains as to how their human cargo should be quartered. Some were "loose packers" and some were "tight packers." The loose packers carried relatively few slaves and reasoned that the additional room allotted each slave insured better survival. The tight packers crammed as many Negroes as they could aboard the ship and believed they would land more live slaves after the inevitable mortality had taken its toll.

On some vessels, the ship's carpenter constructed two wooden shelves within the six-foot-deep hold with a resulting twenty inches of headroom above each shelf. The slaves were manacled, ankle to ankle, and lay on the shelves throughout most of the voyage. The most well-known slaver today is the *Brookes;* the sketches showing how the slaves were packed in her hold appear in practically every modern book dealing with the subject. She is recorded as carrying 600 to 610 slaves across from Africa until the "humane" laws of 1788 restricted her to a cargo of no more than 454 slaves.

Deck grating and a few small ports provided the only ventilation in the cargo hold on the slave ships. In rough weather, however, these openings were covered with canvas to keep the storm-whipped seas from flooding the holds. The intense heat generated by the slaves packed in the holds is said to have sometimes caused steam to rise from under the canvas coverings.

Sanitary facilities below decks were almost nonexistent. On well-run slavers, the sailors swabbed out the slave quarters daily and fumigated them by sprinkling with vinegar. On poorly run slavers, the quarters might never be cleaned except at the end of the Middle Passage when the cargo had been discharged. A slave ship could be detected by its smell "five miles downwind," as one skipper put it.

In the late afternoon, when they were stowed for the night, the slaves sometimes began a wailing "a melancholy noise, expressive of deep anguish," reported Dr. Trotter, a ship's surgeon aboard a slaver. The sounds might continue through the night, as the Negroes cried aloud in despair.

Captain John Newton had commanded slavers, but unlike many of his contemporaries he was considered a just man. In later life he thought back on the traffic in human misery and the degrading effect it had on the officers and crews of the slavers, and said that the trade "gradually brings a numbness upon the heart, and renders most of those who are engaged in it too indifferent to the sufferings of their fellow creatures."

The slave ships of the Yankee traders were a familiar sight in the various slave ports along the Gulf of Guinea. The ports—with their modern names in parentheses—included: Sierra Leone (Freetown, capital of modern Sierra Leone), Cape Coast Castle on the Gold Coast (Cape Coast, Ghana), and Brass and Bonny, on the delta of the Niger River, and Lagos (all now cities in the nation of Nigeria).

Slaves from the Guinea coast were said to be the most tractable and best workers. Negroes captured north or south of the Guinea coast did not survive well in slavery; many died from a variety of diseases and quite a number committed suicide or simply "pined away." According to Daniel Mannix and Malcolm Cowley, slave mortality on the Middle Passage was about 12½ per cent. Another 4½ per cent died in the harbors before they were sold, and 33 per cent died during the "seasoning process." Thus, for every two slaves bought on the Guinea coast, only one was added to the labor force in the New World, an actual mortality rate of 50 per cent.

When the Africans landed in the West Indies they found the climate not too much different from their former homes. Beyond that, however, it was simply another nightmare that differed only in kind from the nightmare of the passage by ship. The food offered them was like nothing they had known before. If any had eaten fish before, it had been fresh or perhaps smoked. But dried salt cod was an ideal food for the slaves on the West Indies sugar plantations as far as the plantation managers were concerned. Great quantities could easily be shipped in the coasting vessels or aboard slavers making the first leg of the Golden Triangle. It kept well in the heat of the tropics and it was cheap.

On some of the sugar islands the slaves were able to grow all of their own vegetable foods, including yams and plantains. But throughout the islands, whatever animal protein the slave got—salt cod mostly, with an occasional treat of salt beef—had to be imported from the far northern Atlantic countries.

We have little information about how the slaves received the salt cod in their diet (in the philosophy of the day, do you ask a horse how it likes the hay?). The planters, however, felt they were doing the slaves a great Christian service. In 1763, an Englishman wrote that the African Negroes "live hardily; so that when they are carried to our plantations (as they have been used to hard labour from their infancy) they become strong, robust people, and can live upon the sort of food the planters allow them; which is, bread made of Indian corn, and fish, such as herrings and pilchards sent from Britain, and dried fish from the North America, being such food as they lived upon in their own country. Indeed they live better in general in our plantations; and they are always ready, on the arrival there, to go to the hard work necessary in planting and manufacturing the sugar cane."

In the late eighteenth century, the growing antislavery forces in England demanded an investigation of slave conditions in the British West Indies sugar plantations. It disclosed that to feed the slaves "fish of the least desirable grades were imported from the New England colonies; and where this was done the planter acquired a reputation for his great benevolence."

In actual practice, two grades of salt cod were shipped from the New England ports. One "merchantable cod" was shipped principally to Spain, Portugal, and Italy. The other, "unmerchantable cod," also called "refuse cod," was shipped to the West Indies to feed the slaves. By definition, the unmerchantable fish was "sun burnt," "salt burnt," otherwise spoiled in preparation (some probably also was partially decomposed), or dry fish that had first been pickled. To the Yankee traders, the spoiled fish no longer was a source of loss that would have to be thrown away or fed to hogs; it could be sold and yield yet another item of profit for the emerging New England merchant princes.

The volume of cod landed, prepared, and shipped was in the thousands of quintals annually. Goode reports an historical review of the port of Salem, Massachusetts, that showed for the period 1747–48, the merchants "shipped off to Europe 32,000 quintals dry codfish; to W. India Islands 3,070 hogs-heads (at 6 to 7 quintals refuse codfish per hogshead) [thus, 19,955 quintals] for negro provision."

By 1762, there was a reduction in landings of cod and, for some reason not made clear, the balance of the fish grades was reversed. The salt bankers in that year landed in the port of Salem "6,233 quintals of merchantable fish and 20,517 quintals of Jamaica fish." The term "Jamaica fish" probably was a euphemism for the terms "unmerchantable" and "refuse fish." The New England fisheries were booming and the New England ships of commerce—including slave, molasses, salt fish, and, as we shall see shortly, rum ships—were going round and round the North Atlantic with profits piling upon profits. In the decade between 1765 and 1775, ships from Salem carried an annual average of 12,000 quintals of salt cod to Europe at $3.50 and to the West Indies at $2.60 per quintal.

The dry, tough, hard-as-boards slabs of salt cod gave a name to at least one facet of the slave trade: the whips used by stewards on Brazilian plantations to punish the slaves were called "bacalhaus," from the Portuguese name for codfish. The rawhide whip, like its namesake, was tough and hard, and it cut deep wounds on the backs of the laboring slaves.

While the Yankee slave traders were procuring slaves for the sugar plantations, they also shipped some into New England for "domestic" use. Slaves were employed on the whaling, fishing, and trading vessels, probably mostly as cooks, carpenters, and "boys," although it is possible that on the fishing vessels, at least, some were used to man the numerous handlines then used to catch cod. The records show that many slaves proved to be excellent seamen, and as early as 1682 a Negro slave belonging to Peter Cross of Massachusetts was given the responsibility of handling his master's sloop at sea. Entries in ships' logs show that Negroes served aboard fishing vessels out of Marblehead, and in 1724 a Negro on a Boston vessel was killed when a sailyard fell to the deck. The entry for another vessel records that a Negro boatman drowned when a lighter sank off the Massachusetts coast.

The third major ingredient in the lucrative triangular trade was rum (and also the molasses from which it was made). Molasses is a by-product of sugar refining, and G. B. Goode reports that early in the eighteenth century the planters at first discarded the vast quantities of molasses that flowed from the limited refining operations then carried on. Some New England captains took aboard casks of the molasses after delivering cargoes of salt fish and other products to the Indies. The molasses went to Boston and to Newport, Rhode Island, then the rum-distilling center of colonial New England. The Massachusetts towns of Boston, Salem, and Marblehead were fishing ports by priority (they had been in the trade the longest) and by the natural advantage of position (they were closer to the rich cod-fishing grounds of the Gulf of Maine). Newport, also an important and busy seaport but a lesser fishing port, took on the major part of the rum distilling.

Rum had been the first alcoholic liquor manufactured in what is now the United States although it was a West Indies "invention." In 1664, a former Dutch distillery was taken over by the British and began to produce rum. Originally called *rum-bullion* (from the Latin *saccharum*, sugar, and the Dutch, *bulioen*, a mass of precious metal), the liquor is mentioned in a seventeenth-century manuscript (author unknown) entitled "A Brief Description of the Island of Barbadoes," in which the writer states that "in the island they produce rum-bullion, alias kill-devil, and this is made from sugar-canes distilled, a hot, hellish, and terrible liquor."

According to W. B. Weeden, by the beginning of the 1700's, the distillation of rum became New England's largest and most profitable industry and continued so throughout the colonial period. Weeden, a nineteenth-century observer of events, wrote in his *Economics and Social History of New England*, "Negroes [i.e., slaves], fish, vessels, lumber, intercolonial traffic in produce, all feel the initiative and moving impulse of rum." It was not long before the New England distillers became the bankers of the slave trade and the fish merchants became the bankers of the molasses trade.

There were sixty-three distilleries along the eastern seaboard of Massachusetts and thirty in Rhode Island, twenty-two of them in Newport. In addition to the thousands of gallons of rum traded to Africa, vast quantities were consumed at home. It was considered an almost indispensable article aboard many cod-fishing vessels for "medicinal purposes" and to "refresh" the fishermen in the few hours they had from tending their lines or dressing and salting fish.

According to Mannix and Cowley, the rum distilleries of Massachusetts were turning out the raw, fiery stuff in a near-endless stream. In about 1750, they annually took in some 15,000 hogsheads of molasses from which they distilled about 12,000 hogsheads of rum. The liquor produced was a heavy, dark drink, thick with the taste and smell of the raw molasses. Even today, a few distilleries still produce what is known as New England rum, but it is a pale ghost compared to its ancestor of the slave-trade days.

Rum is defined as a liquor fermented from a "wash" of "scum, molasses, water, and dunder." Juice pressed from sugar cane is steam heated and the scum—dirt, bits of cane, and other foreign matter—floats to the surface of the hot juice. The scum is removed leaving the clear sugar solution. The sugar solution is heated to drive off excess water, the sugar crystals removed, and the remainder, mostly molasses, added to the scum in the still house. The other ingredient in this witches' brew is the dunder, a viscous mass that remains in the bottom of the still from the previous distillation. To further promote fermentation, the fibrous part of the crushed cane is added to the whole mess.

The wash works for six to twelve days, during which time micro-organisms perform those wonders of biochemistry that change the sugars to alcohol. When the fermented wash is ready, it is pumped into a pot still and the alcohol distilled off. A little flavoring of the wash and cutting with water complete the process. In the days of the slavers rum was cheap to produce since it was made mostly from waste materials left over from sugar production.

The New England merchants very successfully juggled the salt fish-slaves-rum (and molasses) trade and many of them laid the foundations of present-day fortunes. The names of those engaged in the various facets of the trade read like a veritable "Who's Who in New England"; the Pepperells, Malbones, Vernons, Ayraults, and Collins families were at one time engaged in one leg or the other of the Golden Triangle. Even Peter Faneuil of Boston, whose name was given to Faneuil Hall ("The Cradle of Liberty"), took a flyer in the slave trade and made money at it. No stigma was attached to trading in Negroes before the Revolution. The slave trade then was considered to be as honorable a vocation as lumbering or fishing and all were important and valuable New England industries at the time.

The very success of the New Englanders and their industries began to strain the somewhat tenuous relationship between the American colonies and the British rulers some 3,000 miles away. The tail was wagging the dog, and the British did not like it. The Yankees had seen their opportunities and used them well. Yankee ships were everywhere on the world ocean and, as Alan Villiers puts it, "In truth, the real spirit of merchant adventure shifted across the Atlantic." The English had long been successful on the high seas and wanted to keep it that way, and so they began to exert restrictive measures against the new, virile adventurers. The trade from the cod fishery alone furnished the northern colonies with nearly half their remittances to the mother country in payment for articles of British manufacture, "and was thus the very life blood of their commerce." But the colonists had begun trading directly with other nations, to cut out the middlemen, and this brought about restrictive measures.

One of the first of these was the so-called Molasses Act passed by the

British Parliament in 1733, designed to break up the trade between the northern colonies (New England, mostly) and the French, Dutch, and Spanish West Indies islands. The British insisted that molasses for the New England rum distilleries must be carried in British—not colonial—ships. Passage of the act, the colonists replied, would mean failure of the fisheries if they could not sell salt cod directly to the planters and import molasses "to be manufactured into spirit for domestic consumption and for trade with the Indians."

The British continued their fiscal pressures on the American colonists but the Americans continued to fish for cod and trade it for sugar and molasses. A steady stream of pamphlets from the more articulate colonists set forth the position of the Yankee traders, and in December 1763 a group of Massachusetts merchants drew up "A Statement of the Massachusetts Trade and Fisheries" which declared that sugar and molasses were the main ingredients of the slave trade and any duty imposed upon these articles would ruin the fisheries, cause the destruction of the rum distilleries, and destroy the slave trade. Further, it would throw 5,000 seamen out of work and would cause almost 700 ships to rot in idleness at their wharves. The British replied by passing the Sugar Act in 1764, which was designed primarily to actually collect the duties on sugar and molasses imports into the Colonies. The Molasses Act had established the duties but little had been done to collect them.

The harassment of New England fishermen by British men-of-war was also a contributing factor to the American Revolution, and during the war fishing declined dramatically and the slave trade from Yankee ports practically ceased. But there was something new in the wind; the abolitionist movement had gained considerable strength in the northern colonies, and with the end of the war the Yankee merchants found their salt cod was a more lucrative cargo than a boatload of slaves. One of the concessions won from Great Britain by the Americans was the right to cure (sun dry) fish on certain shores of eastern Canada. The ship owners now were more willing to listen to the humanitarian pleas of the abolitionists since Yankee ships—by the terms of the peace treaty—were free to fish and also carry the produce of their trade directly to the West Indies.

On the other side of the Atlantic, British abolitionists also began to press for an end of slavery in British possessions. But once again the proslavery forces erected the bogeyman of ruination of the fisheries, and the West Indies sugar plantations, if slavery were ended. A petition was presented to the House of Commons in 1789 by the pro faction, as follows:

A Petition of the Merchants, Adventurers, and Traders, of the City of Bristol, to the Islands of Newfoundland, was likewise presented to the House, and read; Setting forth, That the Petitioners are much alarmed at a Motion, they hear is intended to be made in the House, for the total Abolition of the Slave Trade, and are hereby induced to represent, that, among the many other Injuries this Kingdom would sustain therefrom, the most valuable Branch of Commerce and great Nursery of Seamen, the Fishery of Newfoundland, would be most materially affected as the Annual Export of Dry Fish from Thence to the West India Islands is very considerable, and, if stopped, would prove fatal to the said Fishery; And therefore praying, That the House will not suffer any Bill to be brought in for the total Abolition of the Slave trade, but only for such Regulations as the House shall deem right.

But humanitarianism prevailed in both Old and New England and, despite the gloom-mongers, the fisheries continued to prosper. By 1790, all the New England states had abolished both slavery and the slave trade. Old habits are not easily eliminated, however, especially if they are tied to the lure of dollars, and there were many diehards, including, for example, the owners, captain, and crew of the ship *Ann* that sailed from Bristol, Rhode Island, in 1806, bound for the Gold Coast of Africa to trade for slaves. Her cargo consisted of "184 Hogsheads, 26 Tierces, 29 Barrels and 4 Half Barrels new Rum, 16 Boxes Claret Wine, 6 Hogsheads Cod-Fish, and misc. stores."

Presumably the *Ann* was successful in her venture and brought a black cargo across the Middle Passage to the sugar islands or to one of the southern states. Nor was she the last American ship to engage illegally in the slave trade; it took the Civil War to end the Yankee involvement.

With the end of the slave trade, and slavery, the British sugar islands in the West Indies fared as poorly as the gloom-mongers had said they would. The Golden Triangle had been balanced precariously on its three legs, and it collapsed when the one leg of slavery was removed.

In a descriptive narrative of the history and economics of the West Indies, James Rodway wrote: "In 1807 a great difficulty had come upon them [sugar planters] by the abolition of the slave-trade, which at once put a stop to all extensions, either in the way of new plantations or of the acreage under cultivation. This was the first great check, and with the fall in prices, which ensued when Britain became the consignee of almost every settlement, caused a cry of 'Ruin' to arise."

And it was ruin indeed. The sugar islands of the British West Indies colonies were producing more sugar than the mother country could use—some 150,000 hogsheads more annually, according to Rodway. As a result, the price fell to half of what it had been and many of the plantations foundered. The end of slavery in the British colonies in October 1886 sounded the death knell of the great sugar plantations. The plantation owners had favored slavery because only with the forced labor of the Negroes could the vast acreage of sugar cane be cultivated and harvested. They foresaw ruination of the sugar economy—and themselves—with the end of slavery, and they were right.

Although the trade complex of codfish, rum, and slaves collapsed, the impact of salt codfish on the West Indies has lasted even to the present. Despite the fact that excellent edible fishes swim in the nearby tropical waters, many shops in Caribbean towns stock salt cod for sale as a staple in the diet of the islanders. A favorite local dish on the Island of Jamaica is *akee* fish made by boiling the yellowish meat of the *akee* fruit pods (first brought from Africa in 1778) and mixing it with salt cod, tomatoes, and onions. But, with New England no longer producing the salt cod, the imports come mostly from Newfoundland and Norway. The Canadian Atlantic Salt Fish Commission reports that in 1963 (their most recent data), Canada sent 33,000 metric tons of salt cod to the Caribbean islands to supply part of the 77,000 metric tons imported that year by the sugar islands. About 21,000 metric tons, according to the Food and Agriculture Organization, went to the island of Jamaica.

Turn-of-the-century dory fishermen at work, hauling in the line, above, and returning to the schooner with their day's catch, below. (*Columbian Rope Company*)

9

Lone Men in Frail Dories

THE AMERICAN REVOLUTION HAD a heavy impact on the New England cod fishery. Some of the fishermen left their trade to become seamen in the new navy, some became privateers, and many simply pulled their vessels up on the shore and did not venture out to the banks while the hostilities were on. The little vessels that did venture to the offshore New England banks or made the long journey north and east to the Grand Bank of Newfoundland were in great peril. British men-of-war stopped many of them, impressed the fishermen, and sank their ships. In return, the New England privateers harassed Canadian vessels fishing their offshore banks.

The end of the war brought the fisheries into prominence. They became an item for negotiation in the drawing of a treaty between Great Britain and the new United States. John Adams was appointed Minister Plenipotentiary in 1779 to negotiate the peace treaty and an agreement for commercial relations. The Congress charged him with very specific duties in respect to the fisheries, noting that "it is essential to the Welfare of all these United States that the Inhabitants thereof, at the Expiration of the War should continue to enjoy the free and undisturbed exercise of their common right to fish on the Banks of Newfoundland and the other Fishing Banks and Seas of North America preserving inviolate the Treaties between France and the said States." If the new nation was to establish itself firmly in the world of commerce as an equal of England, France, and Spain, it must make a bold move by drawing up the strongest sort of treaty. Furthermore, the New England fishermen depended on the markets of Europe as an outlet for their salt cod, and the Grand Bank fisheries were the only ones able to supply the volume of fish needed. Without the fish America had little to offer in exchange for the manufactured goods from Europe so badly needed in the new American economy.

The treaty of peace was signed in Paris in 1782, and Congress ratified it in April 1783, proclaiming a formal end to the hostilities. The treaty gave to the new nation all the territory between the Allegheny Mountains and the Mississippi River and, as John Adams had been charged, gave the Americans fishing rights off the Canadian coast on the Grand Bank and other banks of Newfoundland and in the Gulf of St. Lawrence. Americans were not allowed to dry fish on Newfoundland soil but they were given "liberty to dry and cure fish in any of the unsettled bays, harbours, and creeks of Nova Scotia, Magdalen Islands and Labrador, so long as the same shall remain unsettled."

The prohibition against drying fish on the shores of Newfoundland posed a problem to the American fishermen who made the strenuous journey by sail to the Grand Bank. It meant they must take their boatload of wet-salted fish back to New England and dry it there. Instead of embarking on a fishing campaign of six months or more, they could only fish for a month or so before they had to sail back home with their "trip" of salt cod.

The interpretation of the treaty erupted into a semantic argument about whether the Americans were to have the *right* or only the *liberty* to fish there. On November 29, 1782, John Adams wrote in his diary, "Mr. Stratchey proposed to leave out the Word Right of Fishing and make it Liberty. Mr. Fitsherbert said the word Right was an obnoxious Expression." Adams had worked too long in the struggle for liberty to misunderstand this distinction; now was the time to make it abundantly clear that Americans had the *right* to enjoy the abundance of the productive fishing grounds off the Canadian coast. He rose in the assembly hall and addressed the treaty delegates.

Gentlemen, is there or can there be a clearer Right? In former Treaties, that of Utrecht and that of Paris, France and England have claimed the Right and used the Word. When God Almighty made the Banks of Newfoundland at 300 Leagues Distance from the People of America and at 600 Leagues distance from those of France and England, did he not give us as good a Right to the former as to the latter? If Heaven in the Creation gave a Right, it is ours at least as much as yours. If Occupation, Use, and Possession give a Right, We have it clearly as you. If War and Blood and Treasure give a Right, ours is as good as yours. We have been constantly fighting in Canada, Cape Breton and Nova Scotia for the Defense of this Fishery, and have expended beyond all Proportion more than you. If then the Right can not be denied, Why should it not be acknowledged? and put out of Dispute? Why should We Leave Room for illiterate Fishermen to wrangle and chicane?

Adams' argument was thus simple: the Grand Banks are closer to the United States than to Europe, therefore U.S. fishermen have as great a right to fish there as do European fishermen. A skilled logician might have been able to demolish Adams' argument but the men he was dealing with were statesmen who frequently dispensed with logic in favor of the give and take of international diplomacy. His argument prevailed.

At home, the new American government also was doing all it could to foster the fishing industry. Congress recognized the importance of the salt cod trade. An import duty of six cents per bushel had been imposed on salt coming into the United States. The 1st Congress of the United States gave the fishing industry (a heavy user of salt) relief from the import duty by paying fishermen five cents for each quintal of dried fish and five cents for each barrel of pickled fish exported. The 2nd Congress was even more direct in the support it gave the industry, abolishing these payments and in their place establishing a direct subsidy to boat owners and fishermen based solely on the tonnage of the individual vessel.

At the beginning of the nineteenth century, the fisheries entered a period of expansion and change. A slow recovery followed the decline brought about by the war years, but by the early 1800's American fishermen were actively exercising their new treaty rights on the rich cod grounds in the Gulf of St. Lawrence and off Labrador. Other ships pushed the fishery on the Grand Banks. Coastal towns in New England sent every able-bodied man and boy to the cod fishery. They were gripped with a sort of madness in their zeal to gather the finned gold that Europe and the sugar islands of the Caribbean were eager to buy. Between 1790 and 1810, about 1,232 New England fishing vessels set forth each year, about half of them headed for the Grand Banks and the other half for the north, to the Bay of Chaleur and Labrador. The vessels on the Banks carried 4,627 men and boys and made three trips a year; the vessels that went to the Bay of Chaleur and Labrador carried 5,832 men and boys and made only one trip each year.

In the northern waters, especially off the Labrador coast, the men knew great cold and discomfort. Drifting icebergs were a menace to the ships, but because the men fished from the decks of the main vessels the summertime fogs that are a feature of the area were not yet the "gray terror" they would be to the next generation of fishermen operating from dories. But the sudden gales that swept out of the north, or the side storms that spun off tropical hurricanes, wreaked havoc on the small ships. Under the pounding of the northern sea, the hemp cables that anchored the ships sometimes frayed and parted with a crack like a rifle shot. The vessels were well built and sturdy but sometimes a seam started in the hull and the vessel sank beneath the waves with all hands. Other ships were driven on the rocks of the bleak coast and there pounded until the stout timbers and planking broke up. Some of the worst of these storms are still remembered in small New England towns that lost nearly all their fathers and sons in one great gale of wind. I have walked through the cemeteries of some of these towns and read on headstone after headstone such inscriptions as: "In memory of Enoch Nickerson, lost at sea August 14, 1805 aboard the vessel Martha T. on the Grand Bank."

When a sea disaster struck a fishing community, friends and neighbors rallied to help the families of the lost fishermen. They raised money to pay rents on homes or to buy food, warm clothes, and coal or wood for heating and cooking. Eventually, the welfare programs were formalized as Aid Societies, some of which survive today. John G. Olsen, Jr., disbursing agent for the 105-year-old Gloucester Fishermen's and Seamen's Widows and Orphans Aid Society reported that in 1969 the society gave $7,465 to fifty-five widows in the city. The society was organized in 1865 after a storm on the Grand Bank sank sixteen Gloucester schooners and took the lives of 140 fishermen. The disaster left seventy-five widows and a hundred fatherless children. About $8,000 was raised during the first year after the tragedy, and today the capital fund of the society amounts to nearly $190,000.

Not all of the fishermen were upstanding sons of proud New England villages. Many were the dregs of the waterfront who had to be kept under the watchful eye of the skipper if he was to get any work out of them at all. If the men did not put all their efforts into fishing, the trip might be a "broker"—that is, the value of the catch would not even repay the costs of outfitting the ship for the trip. The owners, of course, would not get the profit they expected and their wrath would be brought down on the skipper, whom they held directly responsible for the success of the voyage. In 1853, Lorenzo Sabine, in a report on the American fisheries for the U.S. Treasury Department, said of one New England skipper that "the fear of making a 'broken voyage' kept him awake and at his post full twenty hours every day throughout the time employed in taking fish."

The early manner of catching the cod was sheer drudgery to the fishermen. In fair weather or foul, in summer fog or icy winter gale, they stood at the rail of the ship and fished with handlines, bundled as best they could against the weather. The lines were of stout hemp or cotton, sometimes tarred to keep them from rotting. They had a heavy sinker to drag them into the depths, and several baited hooks. Each man held two or more lines and jigged them up and down to attract the fish. When a fish was hooked, the long, dripping-wet line was hauled up, hand over hand through a hundred or more feet of water, to retrieve the catch. Mittens were used in the cold months but everything was always wet and a chilling breeze could make it seem as though nothing in the world was dry or warm.

After his fish landed on deck, the fisherman cut out its tongue and strung it on a wire. The tally of cod tongues at the end of the day represented the man's catch and his share of the profits.

When fishing was over, the work day was not yet ended. The fish still had to be dressed and salted down in the hold. Moving like automatons, the weary fishermen gutted, beheaded, and split the cod. During the day the young boys who were part of the ship's complement had been preparing fish as best they could, but the bulk of the catch still awaited the fishermen.

The cod were dressed and split, washed clean of blood and offal, and passed down to the salter in the hold. Working under such conditions for long hours, it is no wonder that from time to time fishermen resisted the system. One such resistance is described by Raymond McFarland, a Gloucester writer who tells the tale in the words of John Perkins, a fisherman.

"Up with the anchor," the skipper shouted down the gangway one morning. "We'll find fish if we have to go to Iceland."

That's how we went roaring to Le Have. We found fish, there, sir, great pot-bellied sons-o'-guns as I never laid eyes on before. Days and days we dragged our lines pulling in codfish and halibut. Did it matter if the wind blew from the no'theast all day? Never. We had to stick to our lines. If the snow pelted us and made us look like Santa Clauses? Never a bit. We stood at the rail, skipper there first and the last to coil in. But trouble was brewing all the time. Men can stand just so much, then the whole thing palls on them.

One day the trouble came. A fellow by the name of Tinker was at the bottom of it, him and a cousin of his and a man from South Boston. Tinker didn't show up at the rail. It was a bitter day, not fit for any man to fish. Skipper looked along the rail and noticed Tinker's place was empty. Bymeby he asked if the man was sick. Nobody answered, except to shake his head. Then skipper went below to find out things for himself. Every man at the rail took a half-hitch in his lines around a belaying-pin to see what was going to happen. Skipper found Tinker in his bunk, smoking his pipe. He's a . . . pretty tough sailor for any man to tackle.

"What's the matter, Tinker? Are you sick?" the cap'n says.

"Naw!" the fellow says, tough-like and blowing the smoke in the skipper's face.

"Too sick to work on deck?"

"Me sick? I don't get that way, sonny."

"Then why not come on deck and do your part?" skipper asks quiet-like. All the men had left their lines and were listening at the gangway to what was going on below.

"I jest don't want to, that's why," Tinker says.

Thud! Just like that!

What happened? The skipper yanked the man out of his bunk quicker than a loon can dive. Then the two went at it, tooth and nail. Things were getting smashed up besides the fighters when the cook took a hand.

"You men can do your fighting on deck. No place for that down here," he said. The cook is always boss of his fo'c's'le, and

Tinker knew he'd be fighting two men if he stayed there any longer, so he made a dash for the gangway to get on deck ahead of the cap'n.

"Come on mates. Now's our time to skin this cursed Down East skunk," he called out to us. Some of the men had been planning just plain murder for him. When he got on deck three men were waiting for him with long fish-knives in their hands. Holy mackerel, wasn't he mad at sight of them. He sized things up at a glance, seeing only three of the crew against him. He jumped back from the companionway to have more room, and grabbed up a capstan bar. That is about four feet long, made of oak. Don't think the skipper waited for the rascals to get him. He rushed right at them, swinging the terrible club back and forth like it was in the hands of a gorilla. Down went one man with the bar smashing into his side. The second fellow leaped aside, trying to come at the skipper from behind. The cap'n swung around to him sudden-like and caught him right across the stomach. Lord, what a groan he let out of him, and doubled up like a jack-knife. Tinker didn't dare to come on. He saw the game was up and ran to the rail where a dory was tied alongside. He jumped into the boat and was reaching up to cut the painter when Captain John reached over the rail and grabbed him by the scruff of the neck. May the Lord roast me as a sinner if it isn't so, sir, he threw Tinker right clean over his head onto deck where the man landed on the main-hatch. Tinker didn't move a muscle after he struck. They carried him below, the crew did, and for three days he was in awful shape.

Well, sir, we stood at our places after that, never a man letting a whimper out of him.

Anyone in the twentieth century who still harbors illusions about the simple, uncomplicated life of the "good old days" needs only to contemplate the working life of the farmer or fisherman in the early nineteenth century. These two occupations represented the principal fields of work open to the average man of the times. It is academic to argue which occupation was more grueling, but it is obvious that the fisherman's life, unlike the farmer's, was in danger from the moment his ship left the harbor until it tied up weeks or months later. Commercial fishing is still a rugged way of life, but in the days of the handliners it took a tough man to withstand the rigors of bank fishing and a tough skipper to lead his crew.

The early nineteenth-century New Englanders introduced new fishing methods that added more danger to the trade. One of these took the fishermen off the vessel and into twelve-foot dories to work their handlines. In this way the fishermen could operate over a wider area than they could when all the men fished from the large vessel. Also, the fishermen believed that the heads, bones, and other offal discarded from the vessel "soured the bottom" and drove off the cod. Under the new system the men in dories could move a half mile or more away from the vessel and fish their handlines on "clean bottom."

The dories were nested in two stacks amidships on either side of the main deck of the vessel. Each morning on the fishing banks, before sunup, the small fleet of dories was launched from the mother ship and each afternoon it returned to the mother ship, where the fish were unloaded and the dories hoisted back aboard. In good weather the dories would be tied up to the ship to float alongside during the night. After the dories returned, the men had to fall to and clean the catch and salt it down below in the hold.

Another change came in the 1850's when some of the vessels began to fish with a "bultow," or line trawl, a long line with a series of baited hooks attached at intervals. Now instead of working a few handlines with perhaps a dozen baited hooks, a fisherman could set a bultow with several hundred baited hooks. The gear had been developed by the Dutch in 1770, and was then taken up by the French, who gave it to the Americans. At first, the bultow was set from the mother ship but soon the dories were put to use to set the gear and haul it back.

The bultow was not universally accepted by American fishermen but those who did use it found it greatly increased their catches, which began to worry the fishermen who were still using handlines. In 1852, M. H. Perley, a Canadian government fishery expert, recorded the complaints of Canadian fishermen who objected to the Americans using the new gear in Canadian waters because they were certain the stocks of cod soon would be depleted. A move to have the bultow banned came to nothing.

At home, some American fishermen also voiced complaints about the bultow. The gear, they said, would cause a school of cod to desert the grounds because fish that tore loose from the hooks would frighten others away. As late as 1877 a group of 137 fishermen from Block Island off the coast of Rhode Island submitted a petitition of protest to the U.S. Fish Commission, claiming that the cod, "suffering from the lacerations of the hook, and fearful of becoming again entrapped, . . . communicate their fears to their sympathizing companions."

The bultow dominated the fishing scene for the next half century or so, a period that is probably the most colorful in the American fisheries. This was the fishery that Rudyard Kipling described in *Captains Courageous*. Lone men in frail dories set out from the schooner each morning to set their lines and return with a fare of fish. This was the time when the talents of the captain of the schooner came to the fore. He sailed his ship out to the banks with only a compass heading and his instinct to guide him. After a certain number of days of speeding with all sails set in a favoring breeze, he calculated that he had put the vessel over the general area of the bank—Georges Bank, 150 miles east of Boston; Browns Bank, south of Nova Scotia; Le Have Bank, Roseway Bank, or Banquereau off the eastern coast of Canada; or Grand Bank off Newfoundland. Wherever it was, the captain then had to find out of the vessel was over cod bottom.

As step one, he had to find out "how much water they had," that is, how deep it was. This called for the use of a sounding lead with a line marked in fathoms.

The second step was accomplished along with the first. A gob of tallow or lard was daubed in the hollowed-out bottom of the sounding lead, and when the lead struck the ocean floor the fat picked up a small sample of the bottom. A mud bottom, the captain knew, was virtually a desert. Few fish, or poor-quality fish like the red hake, were found over mud. A fine-sand bottom might mean haddock, which were useless because they didn't take salting. A coarse-sand bottom, and especially sand with bits of shell in it, was cod bottom, and here they might find their fish.

But there were other considerations in deciding where to fish. Kipling described the thinking process of a typical (though fictional) salt-banker captain, Disko Troop, skipper of the Gloucester dory schooner *We're Here*. Troop drew on all his experience, and the experience of other dorymen before him, to judge where on the bank the cod might be concentrated. "Disko Troop stared forward, the pipe between his teeth, with eyes that saw nothing," wrote Kipling. "As his son said, he was studying the fish—pitting his knowledge and experience on the

Banks against the roving cod in his own sea. . . . [He] thought of recent weather, and gales, currents, food supplies, and other domestic arrangements, from the point of view of a twenty-pound cod; was, in fact, for an hour, a cod himself, and looked remarkably like one."

If the captain's instinct and judgment told him he was in a likely spot, there remained only one final step before serious fishing began. To confirm his judgment, one or more handlines baited with herring or squid went over the rail. A catch of cod on the handlines set the stage for the rest of the month. Here is where the fish were and here is where the dorymen would fish.

Each man went out in his dory every day that the weather allowed. Only gales, rough seas, or fog kept the men on board the schooner to mend gear, swap yarns, or write letters home. On many vessels, Sunday was a day of rest, for most skippers were religious men. The other six days the dorymen went off with their longlines, baited and neatly coiled in tubs, a jug of water and some ships biscuit for emergency food, and a large conch shell to blow as a signal. Some rowed, but others often set a small sail and took advantage of the breeze to move them over the water.

Two men sometimes fished as a team, but just as often they went alone. Once he was away from the vessel the doryman was on his own. He alone decided where he wanted to set his gear. When he reached what he felt was the right place, he set his line. The anchor went over first, with a flagged buoy to bob at the surface at the end of the anchor line. Next went the groundline with its array of shorter lines, called snoods or gangions, set a fathom apart, each with a baited hook attached. When the last of the 500 or so hooks was out, an anchor and buoy marked the end of the string. Now, if the doryman had judged his spot, the tidal currents, and the wind correctly, the cod should soon be taking his bait.

To haul back the gear the doryman had to stand in his tossing little boat and laboriously, hand over hand, pull up the anchor and the groundline. Most hooks would be empty, the bait stolen by some unseen sea creature, and some would have other fish where there should have been cod. There might be several skates, those flattened relatives of the shark; dogfish, small sharks about three or four feet long that even today are the curse of the commercial fisherman; or a cusk or white hake, relatives of the cod that had some value. Once in awhile, there might be a valuable halibut, the largest of all the flounder clan.

[118]

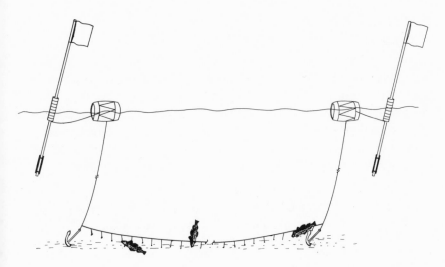

The New England line trawl, as used today, is basically the same as the gear fished by dorymen seventy-five years ago. (National Marine Fisheries Service)

And if all was well there would be enough fifteen- to twenty-pound cod caught by their rubbery lips to fill the schooner's hold and send it skimming back to Gloucester.

With his line in and perhaps a thousand pounds of cod lying in the bottom of his dory, the fisherman set his little sail or pulled on his oars to return to the schooner. Alongside the schooner, the doryman tossed his catch on deck with a long-handled pitchfork. Then the dory was hoisted aboard and nested on the deck. Once the catch was aboard, the work of dressing the fish and salting them down began and continued into the night until every fish was disposed of.

Rudyard Kipling accurately recorded the sights and sounds of dressing cod aboard a saltbanker on the Grand Bank of Newfoundland. Written in 1896, his story in *Captains Courageous* of Manuel, the simple, generous Portuguese-American doryman from Gloucester, gives an accurate picture of the life of toil of cod fishermen. It is evening aboard the *We're Here*, and the crew is dressing and salting the day's catch.

"Hi!" shouted Manuel, stooping to the fish and bringing one up with a finger under its gill and a finger in its eye. He laid it on the edge of the pen; the knife-blade glimmered with a sound of tearing, and the fish, slit from throat to vent, with a nick on either side of the neck, dropped at Long Jack's feet.

"Hi!" said Long Jack, with a scoop of his mittened hand. The cod's liver dropped in the basket. Another wrench and scoop sent the head and offal flying, and the empty fish slid across to Uncle Salters, who snorted fiercely. There was another sound of tearing, the backbone flew over the bulwarks, and the fish, head-less, gutted, and open splashed in the tub.

The fish in the tub of sea water were scrubbed with a stiff-bristled brush to remove traces of blood, slime, and dirt left from the gutting process. No longer looking like a fish, the cod were tossed into the hold where the salting crew was ready.

Down below, the rasping sound of rough salt rubbed on rough flesh sounded like the whirring of a grindstone—a steady un-dertune to the "click-nick" of the knives in the pen, the wrench and schloop of torn heads, dropped livers, and flying offal; the "caraaah" of Uncle Salter's knife scooping away backbones; and the flap of wet, opened bodies falling into the tub.

The schooners had left port with only dry salt in their holds, and now the salt had all been used and the split cod were stacked like cordwood below. The dorymen had "wet their salt" and could return home.

But first there were some social amenities to be conducted. A schooner preparing to return to port made the round of the vessels nearby. Some had only recently arrived on the banks and it would be weeks before their dorymen saw home, so the departing schooners picked up mail and other messages to be delivered to the wives and families waiting ashore. There was a lot of joshing about which was the best ship and which gang of fishermen got the most fish fastest.

Hih! Yih! Yoho! Send your letters raound!
All our salt is wetted, an' the anchor's off the graound!
Bend, oh, bend your mains'l, we're back to Yankeeland—
With fifteen hunder' quintal,
An' fifteen hunder' quintal,
'Tween hunder' toppin' quintal,
'Twix' old 'Queereau an' Grand.

But some dorymen never did get home, and some arrived by circuitous routes months after they had been given up for dead. A sudden shift of wind could swamp a dory laden with half a ton of cod and pitch the doryman into the icy winter sea. Laden down with woolen underwear, shirt and trousers, oilskin jacket and pants, and heavy sea boots, he would sink like a rock. Few fishermen could swim ("Being able to swim is fine if you're fishing in some nice little pond, but when you're out on the Grand Bank in winter—where would you swim to?"). And even if a man could hang onto his overturned dory, the bitter icy seas sucked the very warmth and life out of him in a matter of minutes.

Summer fog—the gray terror—was the doryman's worst enemy, especially to those taking cod on the Grand Bank of Newfoundland, the meeting ground of the warm waters of the Gulf Stream coming up from the south and, from the north, the frigid waters of the Labrador Current and the East Greenland Current. The resulting fog would start as a low, gray cloud on the horizon and then without warning surround the vessel and its tiny fleet of dories, wrapping them in a thick shroud. What had begun as a sparkling, blue-sky day was now a never-never world with nothing visible save the trawl line where it dipped into the sea and a few feet of the sea itself around the dory. Now the doryman must quickly haul in his line and try to row back to the vessel with only his little compass to point the way. Every so often he would place the conch shell to his lips and blast a signal that identified him to his mates and to the schooner. If he was in luck, he would hear the blasts from other dorymen, and, finally, a signal from the schooner. If his compass was faulty, or if he lost faith in its tiny dancing needle, he might row away from the vessel. Some dorymen rowed scores of miles and fetched up on the shores of Sable Island off Canada or (if they were fishing in the Great South Channel west of Georges Bank) on the sandy shores of Cape Cod.

The frigid blasts blowing over the wintry seas heaped the most cruel punishment on the doryman. His life was difficult enough, but the rigors of winter fishing were almost more than a man could endure. The arena in which he worked his art was created, so it seemed, to defeat his every effort. The winter ocean has been described in March 1967 by an editorial writer in *The New York Times:*

The North Atlantic in winter—the world's most savage

ocean—is gray skies and keening gales and blown scud, with ice in the rigging and green water sloshing aboard.

These are the days when the wild seas making up over endless leagues of water rough even the largest liners, when the lifelines are rigged on all weather decks, when the hatches are battened tight, all loose gear struck below or stowed away and the booms snugged against the king posts with an extra turn against the weather.

The sea runs wild from Land's End to Hatteras, its icy breath and charging rollers roil and harry the land, the sand beaches wash out in runnels to the depths, and the very rocks are sundered by the unending assault of tons of water.

Out on the banks, the doryman caught in a freshening winter wind had to act fast. If possible, he tried to haul back the rest of his trawl with its load of fish. But if it was breezing up fast, he had to cut the trawl free and try to get back to the ship with whatever catch he had aboard his tiny craft. With a fair wind to help him he stood a chance of rowing back to the vessel, but with the wind against him he had little chance unless the schooner could make some sail and tack around to pick up her dories.

Many dorymen were lost in sudden winter gales, but some survived in almost unbelievable fashion. One of the most incredible stories is that of Howard Blackburn, a Gloucester fisherman aboard the schooner *Grace L. Fears*. In January 1883, the *Fears* was fishing for halibut on Burgeo Bank some sixty miles south of Newfoundland. He and his dorymate were hauling in their trawl about three miles from the vessel when a breeze sprang up from the southeast. The fishermen didn't mind that at all, because the wind would be behind them when they rowed back to the vessel with their dory load.

But the wind began to increase and snow began to dust down on them, hiding the vessel and the other dorymen from view. Soon the sea was heaped up in foam-topped waves and the snow came down thicker and thicker, driven by the angry wind. Night came on. At first they could see the torch lighted on the vessel to guide them back, but soon the snow obscured that. They rowed and drifted all that bitter cold night, and when daylight came they were alone on the angry tossing sea. Blackburn and Tom Price, his dorymate, decided to row for the land, which they estimated was a hundred miles north.

Blackburn was a bull of a man and he bent to the oars with all the strength he could muster, but Price began to weaken and sat numb in the bow of the dory. By accident Blackburn's thick woolen mittens had been tossed into the sea and his uncovered hands began to freeze, so he took off one of his socks and pulled it over one raw, swollen hand. Because there was no feeling in his hand it was not long before the sock became an icy lump and fell into the sea when Blackburn tried to break the thick rim of ice forming on the gunwale of the dory. By and by his feet became numb too, and the flesh of his hands sloughed off on the handles of the oars. Blackburn realized that his bare hands were freezing, but he made an agonizing decision and kept them wrapped around the handles of the oars so that when they froze solidly he would still be able to slip the rigid claws over the oars and continue to row.

For three days Blackburn rowed the dory into the icy wind, the handles of the oars rubbing against the bared bones in his stonelike hands, and the blood from the raw flesh freezing as soon as it felt the air. Sometime during the second night Tom Price died, and in the morning Blackburn found the frozen corpse sitting in the bow staring at his seemingly useless efforts to cheat the sea.

Blackburn finally made a landfall on Newfoundland and wandered around for a night and a day before he stumbled upon a fisherman's cottage. Here he was nursed back to life, but he lost all his fingers and toes and half of each thumb. Eventually he returned to Gloucester, where generous friends set him up in business with a small tavern.

The dorymen helped bring the cod fisheries of the United States to a new high. Toward the close of the nineteenth century the flourishing industry counted 174 schooners on Georges and Browns Banks alone. In 1879, the equivalent of 92 million pounds of fresh cod was landed by the saltbankers. In 1880, a record was set that has never been equaled when 294 million pounds of cod were landed.

Despite the invention of more efficient catching methods, dory fishing from schooners persisted in New England well into the twentieth century. The last American dory schooner, the *Marjorie Parker*, was setting out her dories to fish with trawl lines on the New England banks in August 1954 when Hurricane Carol put her ashore on the Fairhaven Bridge near New Bedford, Massachusetts. The *Parker* went back to sea later, but as a cruise ship carrying vacationing tourists under sail along the New England coast.

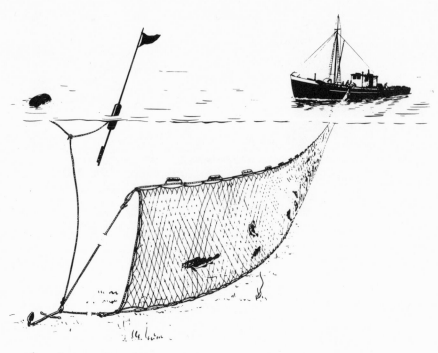

A modern version of the Norwegian gill net, introduced into New England by Spencer F. Baird in 1878. (National Marine Fisheries Service)

Dories are carried today by many of the smaller fishing vessels, not for fishing, but as life boats or utility boats. The line trawl is still very much in use in the American cod fishery. From rocky coves in Maine, from Chatham, Massachusetts, on Cape Cod, and even as far south as Ocean City, Maryland, fishermen put out to sea to set their "strings" of trawl. The small, thirty-five-foot power boats, usually with two-man crews, leave the fishing piers well before dawn for the fishing grounds. Once on the grounds they set lines with the baited hooks in a manner that hasn't changed in over a hundred years.

A minor revolution in fishing gear for the cod fishery was started in 1878 by Spencer F. Baird, first U.S. Commissioner of Fisheries, when he introduced the Norwegian method of fishing with gill nets, walls of netting a fathom or so high and several hundred fathoms long. They are rigged with floats on the top line and weights on the bottom line and are set on the sea floor to intercept the swimming schools of fish. The meshes of the nets are just big enough to let the cod poke its head but not its entire body through the webbing. When the fish attempts to back out of the mesh, the twine catches its gill covers and the fish is gilled (hence the name of the gear).

The nets work best on the heavy inshore runs of spawning fish, such as the winter run of cod on the grounds east of Ipswich, Massachusetts. Handlines and line trawls are not efficient with these fish because spawning cod do not usually feed, and thus few take the baited hooks. Gill nets are still in operation in the cod fisheries, but on a very limited scale, being fished only by a few vessels from Portland, Maine.

In the winter of 1891–92 another kind of gear, the beam trawl, was introduced into the New England fisheries. This was a large cone of netting about twenty-five feet wide at the mouth that tapered back about fifty feet to the cod-end. The beam trawl was towed on the bottom by a wind-driven ship and engulfed any fish that could not swim out of the trawl's path. Beam trawls had been used at least since 1376 to fish in the Thames River estuary in England, and they were widely used in Europe from about the sixteenth century. It was an efficient type of gear for concentrations of bottom fish such as cod, but the operation was at the mercy of the weather: too much or too little wind made it impossible for the vessel to drag the trawl. The hauls sometimes averaged 12,000 pounds of fish, but the netting burst repeatedly when the loads reached 15,000 pounds. Hugh M. Smith, of the U.S. Fish Commission, reported in 1894 that the fishing captains considered the beam trawl a successful type of fishing gear, but most owners of the fishing vessels were not impressed, and few invested money in converting their dory schooners to beam trawling.

Cod hanging from upper rail of sport-fishing boat at Montauk. Below, dressing groundfish, including cod, aboard a large commercial otter trawler. (Albert C. Jensen, National Marine Fisheries Service)

10

Trawlermen and Anglers

THE DAWN OF THE TWENTIETH CENTURY ushered in a new era in American fisheries, and the first decade of the century saw the introduction of techniques which revolutionized the harvesting of cod and other species. Two major changes took place simultaneously. One was the introduction of steam-powered fishing vessels; the other was the invention of the otter trawl.

Now the ships were no longer forced to sit idly, becalmed on a mirror-smooth sea, with their useless sails hanging slack. The fishermen no longer had to clamber about on wet and slippery decks, reefing canvas when the wind blew too hard. And the captain did not have to maneuver the ship about in a series of time-wasting tacks.

Mechanically powered ships took less time to reach the banks and return than did the sailing vessels. Thus, their productive fishing time was greater, and the fresh, iced fish in the hold was sped to market more rapidly. Most important of all, however, the steam trawlers could use more efficient kinds of fishing gear.

Steam trawlers were first used successfully in France in 1876 and in Great Britain in 1881. They were ungainly-looking ships with none of the grace and beauty of the wooden schooners whose lines were almost like those of a sailing yacht. The hiss of the bow wave and the sounds of the wind in canvas were replaced by the "chunk-chunk" of a steam engine. Furnaces fueled with soft coal belched long plumes of black, greasy smoke from a single stack atop the deck house. In later years, old-time fishermen thought nostalgically about the schooners and forgot the hardships they had endured in dory fishing.

The first American steam trawler was the *Spray*, which sailed on her maiden voyage in 1905. Her owners were a group of Boston investors called the Bay State Fishing Company.

Aboard the *Spray* was a revolutionary type of fishing gear, an otter trawl, a vastly improved modification of the beam trawl, developed in 1894 at the British fishing port of Granton. The clumsy wooden beam was discarded and otter boards were attached to each wing. Otter boards (also called otter doors, trawl doors, or, simply, doors) are massive rectangular planked wooden slabs about ten feet long, four feet wide, and four inches thick, bound around the sides with heavy iron frames and fitted on the bottom with thick iron "shoes," like sled runners. The doors are rigged with an iron bridle so that when the net is on the bottom and under tow the doors press outward, like a kite riding up on a breeze, and slide along on their edges. The doors weigh upward of 1,500 pounds and help to keep the trawl on the bottom. Heavy steel cables, three-quarters to seven-eighths of an inch in diameter, are attached to each door, and lead upward to the winch on the deck of the vessel.

The otter trawl is dragged over the ocean floor, tethered by cable or "warp" to the vessel on the surface 300 feet overhead and about 500 to 600 feet ahead. When the otter trawl is fished, a "3:1 scope" is usually employed; that is, the cable hauling the net is about three times as long as the depth of the water. Thus, about 150 fathoms of cable is paid out if the vessel is fishing in fifty fathoms of water. This ratio allows the net to stay on the bottom, and the fishermen say then that the trawl is "tending bottom."

The mouth of the net engulfs fish in its path, and they are concentrated in the narrow cod-end, as they were with the beam trawl. At the end of one, two, or sometimes three hours, the trawl warps are drawn up on the drums of the deck winch and in an intricate series of maneuvers the net is brought alongside and the cod-end hoisted aboard the ship, where its contents are dumped on the deck to be sorted.

The use of the otter trawl changed the manner of operation of the fisherman. When handlining or linetrawling, each fisherman was an individual whose skill and luck largely determined the volume of fish he would catch. In otter trawling, however, the fishermen work as a team, with each man having a more or less specialized role in the operation.

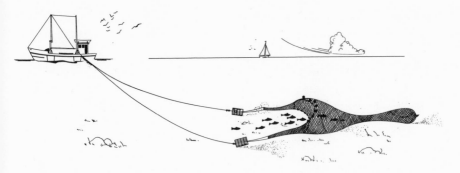

The otter trawl, introduced in the United States in 1905, eleven years after its development in Britain, revolutionized fishing operations. (National Marine Fisheries Service)

Some men are skilled in rigging or mending the nets and so became "twine men," their nimble fingers manipulating the twine needles to fashion a web of intricate knots and meshes. All fishermen must help mend the net when it is badly damaged, but the twine men are especially skilled. Other men operate the controls of the great winches, while one specialist, the cod-end man, ties the peculiar knot that closes the purse-string arrangement of the terminal part of the trawl. At the end of a haul he pulls it open to spill the wriggling wet mass of fish onto the trawler's deck.

When the great net, empty of fish, is once more on the ocean floor, everybody begins to dress the catch. In this operation the men have specialized tasks too, but they still work as a team. Sitting on the massive boards that divide the deck into fish pounds or "checkers," one or two men grasp the fish, belly up, in the left hand, thumb under the mouth and forefinger in its left eye. In two quick motions with a razor-sharp knife (appropriately called a ripper), the throat is cut and the belly laid open. The first cut severs the esophagus, the second exposes the viscera. Now the ripped fish is tossed into the after part of the checker where other fishermen, the gutters, remove the viscera in one easy movement. In almost the same movement, the gutters toss the viscera into another checker and heave the fish into the water-filled wash box set amidships on the deck. Washed clean of blood, slime, and dirt, the fish are picked out of the wash box on the tines of a pitchfork and tossed into the hold where the "hold man" stows them, separated with layers of flaked ice.

The fishermen work in two watches of six hours each, alternating so that each team, or watch, works a total of twelve hours a day, every day, for the ten days or so that the vessel is away from port. This has been the routine for more than fifty years. In 1915, David L. Belding, a biologist for the Massachusetts Commissioner on Fisheries and Game, described steam trawling on Georges Bank:

> The crew consists of a captain, mate, chief and assistant engineer, two firemen, a steward and two crews of six Newfoundlanders—in all 19 men. Each section is alternately on duty for six hours, thus working twelve hours out of the twenty-four. The captain heads one watch, the mate the other, except in stormy or foggy weather, when the services of both are required. A trip usually lasts four to five days, a little over two of which are consumed in running between Georges and Boston, thus giving two to three days of continuous fishing if the weather permits. Night work is carried on with the aid of electric lights supplied from dynamo in the engine room, so that the fishing is practically a continuous process.

Melville J. Fraser, a biologist with the U.S. Bureau of Fisheries, describes trawlermen's meals in 1939. "The food is excellent," Fraser wrote in his diary. "The menu the first evening: pork chops, corn on cob, potato salad, bake potatoes, milk, tea & coffee, homemade biscuits, cookies, watermelon. In addition, the table is always set with food and one can 'mug up' whenever he desires. The crew often goes to the 'galley' and get a cup of coffee and a piece of pie or cake. Some even eat meat and vegetables between the regular meal times."

Today, a generation removed from the days described by Fraser, the food aboard the trawlers is still good and plentiful, and the hungry fisherman is still able to go into the galley for a "mug up" between meals. I have sailed aboard a number of New England trawlers where a typical lunch included roast beef, mashed potatoes, green beans, bread (but not homemade), coffee, tea, or milk, and pie or cake.

Although the food has changed little over the years, the kinds of men that crew the vessels are different. On Belding's ship, half a century ago, the nineteen-man crew included twelve Newfoundland fishermen. In 1939, Fraser reported that the men sailing from Boston included Newfoundlanders (49 per cent), Nova Scotians (27 per cent), native-born Americans (10 per cent), Scandinavians—mostly Norwegians (7 per cent), and a few others. In modern times, the proportion of Canadians in the New England fleets is still high, with two-thirds of the trawlermen fishing out of Boston coming from the Canadian provinces of Nova Scotia and Newfoundland. Six per cent hailed from Europe and the remaining 20 per cent were born in the United States.

Two U.S. Bureau of Commercial Fisheries economists, Dr. Virgil Norton and Morton Miller, reported in 1966 that fishermen in the Boston large-trawler fleet are inclined to follow the sea from a family example. Four out of five of the Boston fishermen have relatives who are, or were, commercial fishermen, usually either father or brother, or both.

The American offshore trawlerman of today is often a descendant of the offshore doryman of yesteryear. A 1964 Bureau of Commercial Fisheries study gives a good composite picture of him. He is fifty-five years old or older, and 20 per cent of his fellows are sixty-five years old or older. He was born in Canada—usually in Nova Scotia or Newfoundland—was probably a fisherman there, but came to the United States because "times were bad at home." His father and grandfather were probably fishermen who practiced their art in a Grand Banks dory. His education is below the national norm: he might have completed grade school but probably did not go on to high school, and a few of his friends (4 per cent) had no formal education at all. He has followed his occupation for over thirty years, and one in five of his companions has at least forty-five years of experience in commercial fishing; two-thirds of them have never worked at any other kind of work and are specialists at their trade.

In the early 1960's, the average full-time trawlerman logged 267 days at sea in a typical year's fishing, and for his labors earned $6,300. Although the annual earnings are on a par with annual earnings in other industries, the hourly wage rates are lower because the trawlermen work an average of 50 per cent more hours while at sea fishing. The hourly wage rate is down to $1.98 per hour on vessels with a seventeen-man crew and $1.71 per hour on thirteen- to fifteen-man vessels. This is not much compensation for working twelve hours a day for a week to ten days at a time exposed to all the vagaries of the weather.

The most arduous task I can think of is dressing fish aboard a trawler on Georges Bank in "a breeze o' wind" at two o'clock on a January morning.

The trawlerman is engaged in a hazardous occupation. There are the obvious dangers: each year one or two of the small wooden ships sinks with all hands during a wintry blow, and sometimes a fisherman is swept off the deck and lost. But there are other less obvious hazards. A piece of rigging may let go while a half ton of fish is being hoisted aboard and strike one of the men on deck. Some men have lost limbs when the heavy steel cables part and whip across the deck like a giant scythe. And more than one trawlerman has had an arm or hand mangled when it was caught in the cable coiling on the drum of the winch. Every year the hazards, exposure, and living conditions aboard the trawlers keep about one-quarter of the fishermen ashore from illness or injury for periods up to thirty-two weeks, and averaging about eight weeks.

Some accidents fall in the incredible category, like the following. A large otter trawler out of Boston was fishing on the Northern Edge of Georges Bank. It was summer and the trip was going along about as usual. Suddenly, however, the trawler radioed that it was sinking, and the crew was taking to the lifeboats. Everyone got off safely and returned to Boston aboard a nearby ship. The story of the sinking caused a number of fishermen to take a second look at their trade and at the twenty-five-year-old vessels in which they went to sea. The ship sank because it was holed by its own otter board. When the forward board was hauled up, it struck the side of the trawler, punching a hole in the steel hull of the ship below the waterline. The hull was a mass of rust, and had the consistency of cheese, so that when the 1,500-pound trawling gear hit the side it went right through.

Another unusual accident had a more grisly overtone. A trawler fishing east of Boston in the Great South Channel in a moderate wind lost one of its fishermen overboard. Someone on deck threw him a life ring, but he was weighed down by his oil skins and boots and disappeared quickly. The captain hauled back the net and steered a search pattern, but to no avail. The drowning was reported to the Coast Guard and the ship resumed fishing. The next day the captain received a radio message from one of the nearby vessels that the body of the missing fisherman had been found. The second trawler had hauled back its net, and when the contents were dumped into the fish pen on deck, out tumbled the body of the drowned fisherman along with several hundred pounds of cod and haddock.

Despite the drudgery of his work and its hazards, the modern trawlerman goes cheerfully about the job he knows best. He feels a great sense of comradeship with his fellow trawlermen, and his greatest compliment is to refer to a chum as "a good shipmate." Any spare moments in the galley or on the bridge standing a wheel-watch are spent in yarning about this ship or that, a particular captain, or how they rode out the "gale o' wind in 19 and 48 aboard the *Thomas Whalen* on the K ground of Georges." (That particular fishing ground is so called because good fishing is found at certain times of the year around the spot where the "K" in Georges Bank is printed on the U.S. Coast and Geodetic Survey navigation chart.)

The ship and their crew mates become the center of fishermen's lives. They are ashore only three days every two weeks, so that "home" is only an interim between fishing trips. In their circumscribed conditions on board ship the fishermen have evolved a unique way of life, including an especially long list of superstitions. The American fisherman's superstitions are a lot like his European counterpart's. It is a sure portent of hard times if someone aboard ship says the word "pig." If mention of the animal must be made, it is called "the square-nosed fellow," "the curly-tailed fellow," or simply "the denizen." On one of his trips, the biologist Melville Fraser unknowingly said the forbidden word. "The fishermen all stated that the next set of fish would be a poor one," he wrote in his report. "The net was hauled in and it was found to contain exactly two fish. The gear was torn and ripped."

The fishermen also warn that "you sing on deck and whistle behind the plow," and they never whistle on board the ship because to do so would be to "whistle for the wind." Anyone foolish enough to break this unwritten rule might call up the furies of a fierce gale, especially the dreaded wintertime nor'easter. One does not bring a black suitcase aboard ship, and it is a sure invitation to bad luck to wear anything but a black sou'wester with a set of oilskins.

The fisherman's working conditions is one reason the industry faces a severe manpower shortage. Fewer and fewer young men care to go to sea aboard trawlers to endure the long hours, hard work, and low pay, so the trawlers are crewed mostly by older men. To compensate, the industry seeks greater automation of the process of catching fish. One step in this direction is the 300-foot *Seafreeze Atlantic*, the first of a radically new line of American trawlers. She is a stern trawler, and requires fewer men to handle the gear. She is also a floating factory with machines to fillet, skin, and freeze the fish on board, reducing the amount of labor required. An important labor-saving device is a "vacuum eviscerator" to eliminate the ripping and gutting process on deck.

The landings of cod in recent years have fluctuated with market demand, and especially with the availability of the fish. New vessels and new techniques should provide increased landings of fish. The comparative landings of two Boston trawlers show why. On September 11, 1968, one of the older vessels, the *Arlington*, landed a total of 99,000 pounds of fish, including 57,000 pounds of cod, 38,000 pounds of haddock, and some pollock and flounder. A few days later, one of the newest vessels, the *Bay State*, fishing on the same grounds, landed 122,000 pounds of fish, including 38,000 pounds of cod, 72,000 pounds of haddock, and some pollock and flounder. In each case, the landings represented one trip.

The historical statistics of the cod fishery portray an industry that has been seriously affected by technological advances and changing consumer preferences. The graph illustrates some changes in cod landings that were caused by technological advances. For example, there was a great rise in landings in 1905–6, brought about by the intro-

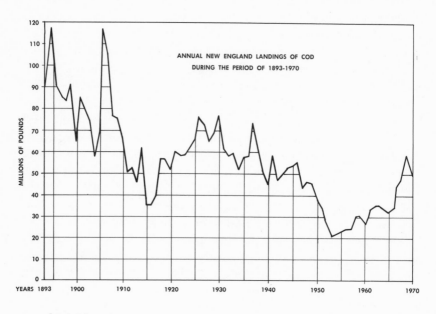

duction of otter trawling with steam-powered vessels. This date was also the beginning of the end of the American salt-cod fishery and the start of the iced fresh-cod fishery. The American housewife was delighted to find she no longer had to soak the fish overnight for Friday's dinner.

The graph shows a dip in landings during World War I, when few trawlers dared risk a torpedo from a German submarine. The industry was revitalized in the early twenties following a brief postwar depression. More trawlers were built, and cod landings boomed along with the rest of American industry in the "Roaring Twenties." This period, however, marked a development in the retailing of fresh fish that toppled cod from its position as the prime New England species. In the autumn of 1921, plants in Boston began to fillet fish and ship the product to retail markets. Before this, only whole fish were sold in the retail market, and they had to be filleted there. Haddock was the first species handled this way, and because the species was abundant it soon cut into the market for cod.

Haddock had always been available to the hook-and-line fishermen offshore, even on the dorymen's "cod grounds." Haddock were usually discarded as so much trash since the flesh is somewhat softer than that of the cod and it does not salt and dry well. The general opinion was expressed by Lorenzo Sabine in 1853: "The hake and haddock are poor fish, and neither commands more than half the price of the cod. . . . The haddock, when fresh, suits the taste of some; but when dried, it is without reputation even in the hut of the negro [slave], who is doomed to be its principal consumer."

But all this was changed by the fresh-fish trade and by later developments. Other trawlers found haddock in great abundance on the relatively smooth, sandy parts of Georges Bank. (Cod favor rough bottom, which cannot be fished by otter trawls without great damage to the nets.) And in Gloucester, Clarence Birdseye's development of a reliable deep-freezing technique made it possible to freeze the haddock fillets, which now moved to the fore and relegated cod to a minor position in the U.S. industry.

During the Great Depression of the 1930's, all U.S. fishing hit a low level. Fleets were tied up and their fishermen joined the ranks of the unemployed, and even those vessels that continued fishing brought in fewer cod because the species was then in low abundance. Fishery biologists were at a loss at the time to explain the scant numbers of cod

[135]

on the formerly productive banks during the past quarter century. The many other variations in cod landings have resulted from a number of factors, both man-caused and natural. In World War II, decreased offshore fishing was the obvious cause of reduced landings. A brief postwar recovery was followed by a decline in production in the early 1950's that biologists believe was the result of an increase in haddock abundance, which diverted trawlermen's efforts. This was followed in the late 1950's by a decline in haddock abundance and therefore an increase in the attention paid to cod. The 1960's have seen a similar seesaw of landings of the two species, and this is particularly striking in the late sixties. The haddock population has been reduced by seven spawning failures in a row, coupled with an increase in catches by foreign vessels. By 1970 the haddock fishery was in a state of collapse. In contrast, there have been several very successful spawnings of cod, and the species is again abundant, especially on the rough parts of Georges Bank. Thus, in 1967–70, more cod were landed by U.S. trawlermen than in the years immediately preceding.

But the amount landed by U.S. trawlers is not enough to satisfy domestic demand. In 1970, 53 million pounds of cod (live weight) were landed by U.S. fishermen, mostly at New England ports. In addition, 96 million pounds of cod fillets (equal to about 300 million pounds live weight) were imported from other nations. Two-thirds of the imports came from Canada, the remainder from Iceland, Denmark, and Norway. In addition to the fillets, nearly 195 million pounds of frozen blocks and slabs (equal to about 600 million pounds live weight) were imported. The blocks and slabs are sawed into pieces and processed in American factories to be sold in retail markets as "fish sticks." Most of the blocks and slabs are made from cod, although a small percentage may be haddock and pollock. Canada again was the principal supplier of the blocks and slabs, followed by Iceland, Norway, and Denmark.

The cod fillets and blocks are part of the 3.7 billion pounds of edible fish imported into the United States in 1970. That same year, 4.9 billion pounds of edible fish were landed by U.S. fishermen.

It is thus obvious that there is a considerable demand for cod on the U.S. market, but that the domestic fishing fleet is able to supply less than a fifth of the 313 million pounds eaten by Americans. Part of the reason the U.S. fleet does not land more cod is that fishermen prefer to harvest the more abundant species such as flounder and, in the past, haddock. On the wholesale market, cod usually brings in half the price received for flounder or haddock.

Another reason for the lower landings of cod is low abundance of the species on the traditional American fishing grounds off the northeast coast of the United States compared to fifty to seventy-five years ago. Cod abundance is greatest in the Gulf of St. Lawrence off Newfoundland, where, in the spring, an otter trawler can take as much as thirty-five tons in a two-hour tow. In contrast, on Georges Bank trawlers catch only about one and a half tons of cod per day. Georges Bank has never been what the fishermen call "good cod country" like the Canadian banks (especially the Grand Bank off Newfoundland), although at times parts of Georges Bank supported a productive fishery. Richard C. Hennemuth, a Woods Hole specialist in population dynamics, believes that the low abundance of cod in New England waters was caused by overfishing.

But perhaps a recent increase in cod abundance is a harbinger of a return of the species to something like its former numbers. A survey by the Woods Hole research vessel *Albatross IV* indicated a large number of cod that were spawned in 1968 (young-of-the-year), promising an increase in abundance in later years as these young fish grow and reach marketable size.

The cod populations off the east coast of the United States are being affected by rising fishing pressure from foreign vessels, and this may have a marked influence on the future of the fishery. Until about 1962, only U.S. and a few Canadian vessels fished the banks off New England. Beginning in that year, great fleets from the Soviet Union began to fish the banks for a variety of species. Other nations soon followed. In 1970, Spanish vessels off the coast of New England caught 7,247 metric tons of cod, the U.S.S.R. caught 364 metric tons, and Polish and German (both Federal Republic and People's Democratic Republic) trawlers landed smaller amounts. That same year, U.S. vessels fishing the same grounds landed 22,039 metric tons of cod.

The heavy fishing of the Soviets and other nations has fishery biologists worried. Seen from another ship, these fleets are impressive, but from the air they are overwhelming. Sometimes more than 200 vessels are involved. During a surveillance flight in a U.S. Coast Guard observation plane I saw a European fleet in operation in the waters off New York. It included ninety-seven vessels, of which seventy-six were Soviet and twenty-one were Polish. The Soviet fleet consisted of two factory stern trawlers, sixty-seven side trawlers, three refrigerated-fish transports, two cargo vessels, and two factory base ships. The Polish fleet consisted of three stern trawlers, fifteen large side trawlers, two supply vessels, and one factory base ship.

Foreign vessels are in the waters off the American coast for three to six months, catching and processing great quantities of fish. The factory trawlers fillet and freeze their own catches and those of the side trawlers. Transports take the processed fish across the Atlantic to the homeland. Crewmen spend up to a half year on the fishing grounds, ultimately returning on one of the homeward-bound transports.

The Soviets and Poles are not the only foreign nations that fish the rich cod grounds off the American coast; they are joined by ships from East and West Germany, Norway, Spain, France, Great Britain, Greece, Japan, Iceland, and Cuba. The total fishing effort is having a marked effect on the stocks of fish. If natural reproduction should fail —as happened in the California sardine in the 1930's and the Georges Bank haddock in the 1960's—there may be another drastic decline in cod abundance, perhaps even a collapse of the fishery.

Since about the end of World War II, sport fishermen from Maine to New Jersey have also made heavy inroads on the stocks of cod. This is nearly a year-round fishery, although most fish are caught during the spring and fall when the cod are moving from one ground to another. Off the Middle Atlantic states of New York and New Jersey, the fishermen concentrate on the New Jersey coastal cod population. These fish over-winter south of New Jersey and spend the summer in southern New England waters. Fishing activity is least in winter when hard weather keeps the small boats in port, and in summer when the fishermen concentrate on silver hake, tautog, scup, bluefish, and striped bass.

Anglers fish from small power boats or, more commonly, from large, commercially operated "open" boats on which fishermen pay $10 to $15 for a day's sport. A typical boat is the *Jess-Lu III* out of Freeport on the South Shore of Long Island, New York. She is an eighty-seven-foot converted Coast Guard cutter. Captain Jay Porter uses elaborate sonar devices to locate sunken ships that act as artificial fishing reefs to attract and concentrate a host of species, especially cod. Captain Porter finds clues to many of the wrecks from commercial fishermen whose otter trawls, dragged over the bottom, snag on the submerged hulks. He sometimes sends scuba (for Self Contained Underwater Breathing Apparatus) divers down to confirm the position of the wrecks, and their location is plotted on a chart that he guards as jealously as a map of a secret tunnel into Fort Knox. If only he knows the location of a productive wreck, the fishermen aboard his ship will be assured of a good catch of cod. His chart includes the location of wooden sailing ships which have been on the bottom for more than a century, as well as those of modern ships like the Italian luxury liner *Andrea Doria* which sank in 1956. Captain Porter knows that "the deeper the wreck, the bigger the fish," and points with pride to a sixty-three pound cod that one of his fares hauled up from 200 feet.

Montauk, "The Cod Sportfishing Capital of the World," is home port for a fleet of anglers' boats that concentrate on codfish all year round. Montauk boats fish a variety of grounds, but the most famous and productive is Cox Ledge, about twenty-two miles southeast of Martha's Vineyard, Massachusetts, and twenty miles east of Montauk. Hugo Uhland, a local newspaper columnist, reported that the Montauk fleet is "into monster cod at the ledge every day. The bottom is virtually paved with fish. Some of the anglers get as many as forty fish. The cod average from five to twenty-five pounds, with lots of thirty to forty-five pounders."

Captain Les Behan, skipper of the Montauk boat *Peconic Queen*, took twenty-eight anglers to another favorite ground six miles south of Montauk, and landed over 600 cod. One man, Charles Carmen, Jr., of City Island, New York, "high hook" for the trip, caught forty-one fish.

There are no detailed statistics of catch for the recreational fishery, as there are for the commercial fishery, but it is obvious that anglers exert considerable fishing pressure on the cod populations. On an average day, a boat out of Montauk lands 4,000 to 6,000 pounds of cod. An estimate of angler catches of cod in the New England and Middle Atlantic states in 1965 was slightly less than 30 million pounds. Catches of Atlantic cod and those of Atlantic tomcod, a smaller relative, are lumped, but tomcod is far less abundant and the largest weighs only about one and a quarter pounds, so that the bulk of the catch can be taken for Atlantic cod. This places the recreational catch of cod only a little behind the commercial catch, which was 46.6 million pounds in that year.

Sometimes anglers tie into really big cod. For many years the record recognized by the International Game Fish Association was a lunker that weighed seventy-four pounds, four ounces, and was sixty-six inches long, caught on June 2, 1960, by James J. Duggan fishing out of Boothbay Harbor, Maine. This fish was overshadowed by the sixty-five inch, eighty-one-pounder caught by Joseph Chesla aboard the *Jamaica* out of Brielle, New Jersey, on March 15, 1967, and even that record was toppled two years later. On June 8, 1969, a ninety-eight pound, twelve-ounce cod was caught off Newburyport, Massachusetts, by Alphonse Bielevich. He was fishing with three companions from a twenty-five foot boat and took the fish on a spinning rod with twenty-pound-test line after a thirty-minute struggle.

It is more than just the chance of catching a big fish that brings out the recreational cod fishermen. The men endure—and cheerfully so, it seems—a variety of physical discomforts to be able to take part in their ocean-going recreation. The boats leave the docks early in the morning, usually between 3:00 and 5:00 A.M. I have fished from the Montauk cod boats alongside anglers from Pennsylvania and New Jersey, as well as from New York City and the local area. Some of them must drive all night to get to the boats on time. The round trip to the fishing ground can take up to eight hours. For example, when the Montauk boats fish Cox Ledge, it takes them about four hours to get there.

Depending on the weather, the trip to the fishing ground may or may not be pleasant. Many of the men sleep on benches or on the floor of the deck house, but if there is any kind of a sea running it can be uncomfortable. Once they are on the fishing ground, the men stand on the pitching deck, heavy fishing rods in their hands, dangling clam-baited hooks on the bottom some 150 feet or so below. During the winter the fishermen are bundled up like Arctic explorers, but in the summer peaked caps and a minimum of clothes is the rule. Spring and fall bring the hordes of pesky dogfish to steal the bait before it gets to the bottom. In the summer, large sharks, porpoises, and an occasional whale liven the marine scene. But it is the cod the men are after.

Some of the anglers feel like they are brothers in a close-knit fraternity. They go out once or twice on a deep-sea fishing expedition and then they are hooked. Even the winter's cold can't keep them away from their cod fishing, and getting up at midnight or 1:00 A.M. to make an early sailing is eagerly accepted as part of the sport.

There is also a sort of gambler's comradeship aboard the boats. In addition to the chance they might not get any fish, there is the chance they might land a really big one, not necessarily one for the record books but one that will take the pool money aboard the ship. The cod fishermen on one boat, for example, pay a $15 fee for their fourteen-hour trip and most of them are glad to pay another $10 or $15 into the pool of prize money. The prizes reach $500 on some trips, with a large share of the money going to the angler who lands the largest cod, another share going to the angler who catches the most cod, and even a consolation prize for the one who catches the smallest cod. Naturally, there are always groans for the fish that get away. Maybe the cod that broke loose before it could be landed would have been the lunker that took the top prize in the pool.

John Cacace of Yonkers, New York, will always remember one cod. On December 28, 1968, fishing aboard the Sheepshead Bay open boat *Helen H. II*, he caught a thirty-four-and-a-half-pound cod. Like many of the other fishermen with him, Mr. Cacace had been contributing to a pool in the Sheepshead Bay Cod and Whiting Tournament. The contest ran for fourteen weeks, and a total of $2,568 had accumulated in the pool. John's fish was the winner; he was awarded a prize of $1,284, making his cod worth almost $38 a pound.

Catching cod on modern New England gill netter. The Soviet base ship Ural, *below, dwarfs the trawler tied alongside to offload its catch. (National Marine Fisheries Service)*

11

The North Atlantic Cod Fishery Today

DESPITE THE HARDSHIP, deprivation, and danger of the life of the deepwater trawlerman, he continues to go to sea to harvest cod in the Atlantic Ocean. Men from a score of nations from both sides of the Iron Curtain catch and land billions of pounds each year.

Most cod are caught in the waters of the northwest Atlantic, particularly on the extremely productive Grand Bank of Newfoundland. The catch there in 1970 was 520,096 metric tons; production from the Nova Scotian banks was next highest, with a catch of 255,703 metric tons. Other landings include 209,801 metric tons from the Labrador banks, 103,994 metric tons from the banks off West Greenland, and 35,387 metric tons from off New England.

In the northeast Atlantic, the banks around Iceland yielded 470,757 metric tons; the Barents Sea, 437,704 metric tons; and the Norwegian Sea, 381,426 metric tons. Other important areas include the Baltic Sea, the North Sea, and the Spitzbergen-Bear Island grounds.

Most of these areas have been fished since ancient times but they have continued to furnish what once seemed to be a never-ending supply of cod. However, there are hints now that there may be a reduction in the resource as a result of overfishing, unwise management practices (nonconservation is one way of expressing it), and pollution of the world ocean by a host of noxious substances.

The cod fisheries are of great importance in the economics of some regions. Newfoundland, a prime example, has been on a "cod economy" for generations. With the Grand Bank literally at its doorstep, this Canadian Atlantic province has always been famous for its dried salt cod. Her fishermen caught 152,795 metric tons of cod in 1970, a fifth of which was salted and dried.

The United States buys a large share of Newfoundland's fresh cod, while nations along the west coast of Africa and in the Caribbean islands are major importers of her salt cod. The salt-cod market declined as a result of the Nigeria-Biafra civil uprising in Africa, and the devaluation of the British pound sterling late in 1967 affected several West Indian currencies and resulted in a loss of other markets for Newfoundland salt cod, notably in Jamaica. The Newfoundland government bought up the resulting surplus supplies of salt cod for distribution to underdeveloped countries which were not normally importers of salt fish from Canada. The World Food Program of the United Nations received about $500,000 worth for distribution, and an additional $50,000 worth went to aid South Vietnamese refugees.

The U.S. market for fresh fish from Newfoundland was weakened in 1966 when the Roman Catholic Church lifted its rule against the eating of meat on Fridays. The decline was first significant among institutional buyers such as hospitals and schools, and gradually spread throughout the general consumer market. The effects of the lifting of the Friday abstinence rule have been reduced in subsequent years. However, while the U.S. market for domestically caught fish has recovered, the U.S. market for Newfoundland fish has not. This left Newfoundland processors with 30 to 40 million pounds of fresh-frozen cod on their hands. In response, the Canadians introduced modern automated machinery and mass-production techniques to lower processing costs, which resulted in a progressively smaller number of people being employed in the industry; small, marginal firms were forced out of business.

The Grand Bank and the fishing grounds in the Gulf of St. Lawrence, immediately south of Newfoundland, have long been shared by vessels from many nations. France, Spain, Portugal, Great Britain, and Germany have regularly sent fleets to harvest the cod for their home markets. In the late 1950's and early 1960's, these fleets were joined by vessels from other nations for the first time. Some of them came because the ancient grounds in the northeast Atlantic and the North Sea were overfished and could no longer provide the necessary volume of cod. The newcomers included the Iron Curtain nations of Poland, East Germany, and the Soviet Union. Great fleets and innovative devices and techniques resulted in greatly increased catches of cod in Newfoundland waters, and instead of providing markets for the Newfoundland catch, these European nations became competitors.

A Soviet fleet may number more than a hundred vessels, which systematically and efficiently sweep the grounds. Medium-sized trawlers, 125 to 178 feet long, are the mainstays of the fleets; some of them include refrigeration and freezing facilities aboard. These ships periodically offload their catches to freezer-transport ships to be returned to the homeland. The most impressive of the Soviet vessels are the 278-foot factory stern trawlers, which in addition to catching fish can process the catch on board, using the fish down to the last scrap. Below decks the ships have complete, automated production lines with machines that behead and fillet the fish. Other machines skin and package the fillets, which then are moved to blast freezers. The inedible parts —skin, bones, and viscera—are reduced aboard ship to meal and oil, the meal to be used in hog and poultry rations, the oil in a variety of industrial products.

The Soviet fleets also include service ships: transports from 250 to 500 feet long for carrying frozen fish, bags of meal, and barrels of oil back to the U.S.S.R.; base ships up to about 500 feet long; tankers; and repair and salvage vessels. The base ships provide medical and dental facilities and, with the transports, bring crews to and from the homeland. Some of the service ships also provide rest and relaxation facilities. Women often make up part of the crews aboard the service ships and the factory trawlers, functioning in a variety of occupations, particularly as workers in the fish production lines below decks. Some also cook and wait on table in the dining salons or serve as ship's doctors, nurses, or barbers on the big ships. The small trawlers are crewed only by men because the living and working conditions aboard these vessels are more primitive.

The Soviet fleets are extremely efficient. A fleet of trawlers from the Baltic port of Kaliningrad fishing on the Newfoundland banks averaged 200 metric tons per day of high-quality cod.

Not all of the Soviet vessels are large, modern trawlers. The Soviets have also launched longliners to fish with gear that is little changed from the kind the Dutch developed in the eighteenth century. A small fleet from the Latvian port of Liepaja fished off Iceland in May 1968 equipped with fifteen kilometers (9.4 miles) of long line, fitted with over 20,000 hooks. Under favorable conditions this gear could catch as much as six metric tons of cod during one haul.

Soviet satellite nations have followed the U.S.S.R. example and have expanded their spheres of fishing activities. Two of the most aggressive are Poland and East Germany. The Poles generally use the same kinds of vessels and tactics as the Soviets, but the East Germans are more innovative. In 1967, East Germany fished the southwestern Atlantic, the mid-Atlantic, and Georges Bank. By early January 1968, over 2,000 East German fishermen were working on these grounds. This expansion was helped by the Soviets, who gave the East Germans data on fishing in those areas and trained them in fishing techniques.

The East Germans formerly depended on the traditional European fishing grounds for cod, but they were forced to look for other areas when the fish became less abundant in 1966 and 1967. In early 1967 ice and severe storms made the Labrador winter cod season a failure, and later that spring the fishing off Newfoundland also was poor. The only solution was to keep moving south, which they did, ending on Georges Bank in midsummer. Later, however, because the stocks were not sufficient to support such heavy fishing pressure, the East Germans shifted their effort to other species and other grounds. They joined the Soviets and Poles in fishing for silver hake and red hake at the edge of the Continental Shelf off New York and New Jersey, and also fished for the very abundant herring, a favorite fish in the European homeland.

The Communist East German government now pursues an economic system similar to that in the U.S.S.R., one that makes "profits" (the value of the goods or services produced in any operation, above and beyond the cost of carrying out that endeavor) more important than volume of production alone. This has affected the fisheries, and the East Germans have equipped their high-seas fishing fleets with Automatic Data Processing (ADP) machinery, including computers, in an effort to increase their efficiency. The vessels carry teletype machines to transmit daily reports on catches, weather currents, and other useful data to the mother ship, where a small computer processes the information and relays it to the home port of Rostock. There a larger computer is programed to guide the fleet to the best fishing grounds and to direct the processing of the catch. The fleet of the Rostock Fisheries Combines includes over a hundred vessels.

While some of the most recent entrants in the cod fisheries, such as the East Germans, have enjoyed success, some of the traditional and oldest participants have had difficulties. Iceland, for example, went through a period during the late sixties when her cod fisheries met disaster. In 1966 the cod catch declined by 18.7 per cent, and in 1967 it declined further by 22.8 per cent, partly because of a decreased abundance of cod and partly because of a diversion of the fishermen to the herring fishery. To strengthen the market for cod, the Icelandic industry turned its processing efforts to products which commanded the highest export value and which had greatest demand on the world market. For example, because of the almost complete loss of the stockfish market in Nigeria in 1967–68, the industry shifted to the production of better-quality frozen and salted cod. A large proportion of the Icelandic frozen cod is exported to the United States, where it sells at a lower retail price than cod caught and processed by U.S. fishermen.

Norway, another traditional participant in the North Atlantic cod fishery, has also been beset by problems. In one recent instance, a man-made problem turned what would have been a natural benefit into a near disaster. According to the periodical *News of Norway*, in the spring of 1968 the sea around the Lofoten archipelago was teeming with spawn-ready cod. The fish were in such abundance that the fishermen made catches twice as large as they had the year before. But the fish curers ashore refused to buy the large catches because they felt the government had fixed the price to the fishermen at too high a level. Further, because Norway's African market for air-dried cod (stockfish) had nearly collapsed, the fish was a glut everywhere on the world market; fish curers in the Norwegian province of Finmark—which is nearly 80 per cent dependent on its fishing industry for income— held large inventories of unsold stockfish.

The apparent abundance of cod in Norway did not reflect the real state of affairs. Fishery scientists who had studied the age composition of the cod in the catches and the abundance and distribution of young-of-the-year cod had arrived at a dire conclusion. Hallstein Rasmussen, Deputy Director of the Norwegian Fisheries Directorate, reported that "rapidly diminishing resources of fish, particularly cod and related species, in the Northeast Atlantic is one big problem for which a solution has yet to be found. Our fishermen seem unable to see beyond the present situation which is one of ample supplies of cod and some marketing problems abroad, notably for stockfish."

Rasmussen went on to describe how scientifically supported predictions of drastically reduced catches in the immediate future seemed to make no impression on the fishermen. Even as the predictions of low abundance were being made, the trawlers were taking large quantities of fish just outside the coasts of Troms and Finmark, since the cod, although their over-all number was low, had concentrated to feed on capelin and had thus provided the Norwegian trawlers with temporarily excellent fishing. At the same time cod fishing was very poor in the other grounds in the Barents Sea.

The most ancient cod fishery in the Northwest Atlantic is the Portuguese Campanha Bachaloeira, which has exploited the Grand Bank stocks continually since the fifteenth century. Even today the Portuguese schooners spend six to nine months on the banks, catching cod for salting aboard the vessels. The fishermen, usually about fifty to a vessel, fish alone in dories. They set longlines baited with herring or squid, or (when these are not available) with chunks of wolffish, halibut, or cod entrails. While the baited hooks are soaking, the fishermen jig for cod with handlines. The schooners fish on the Grand Bank and on the banks close to the west coast of Greenland. This method of fishing and the life aboard a twentieth-century dory schooner are well described by Alan Villiers in his book, *The Quest of the Schooner Argus*.

Since the end of World War II, these motor and sail vessels have been joined by Portuguese otter trawlers. The trawlers have been taking an increasingly larger proportion of the catch. In 1970, for example, Portuguese vessels took aboard a total catch of 162,655 metric tons of cod (split and salted aboard ship) of which 126,871 tons were caught by otter trawlers and 35,784 tons by dorymen from the schooners. The trawler catch no doubt will increase while that of the schooners will decrease. Each year, fewer and fewer of the sons of Vasco da Gama and Prince Henry the Navigator are eager to venture out in their cockleshells of dories to try for the title of "First Fisher" of their schooner or of the fleet. Most of them would rather work the comparatively easier life aboard a salt-cod trawler. But, schooner or trawler, these fishermen still eat the "soup of sorrow," the soup prepared from codfish heads; tradition has it that he who eats the soup of sorrow is doomed to return again and again to the Grand Bank and the cod fishery.

France, Portugal's ancient rival for the Grand Band cod, is still very active in the twentieth century. Her vessels fish for a variety of species, but the cod catch is the most important in quantity and value (about $14 million), more than half of it processed for the salt-fish market. The fishery is conducted on the Grand Bank aboard large otter trawlers that make three-month-long fishing trips two or three-times each year beginning in February and continuing until mid-December. The fish are split and salted aboard the trawlers, following much the same procedures as those on the old sailing ships centuries before.

The French trawler fleet was beset by a crisis in 1969 that threatened the entire French cod fishery. The skippers on the Grand Bank threatened a partial production strike, stating that they would make only one trip a year instead of the customary three. They complained that their vessels could no longer compete with Spanish, Icelandic, and British ships on the Grand Bank because those nations had devalued their currencies. As a result the price dropped from thirteen to twelve cents a pound for salt cod, and from nineteen to seventeen cents a pound for frozen cod, and at the lower values the French fishermen no longer received an equitable wage for their labors. Fisheries economists, however, pointed out that the real problem is that only nine of the thirty-one vessels in the French fleet are modern, capable of freezing cod while operating on the bank.

The competition the French trawler captains complained about was very real, particularly from the Spaniards, who were pressing their cod fishery on the banks of the northwest Atlantic and with innovative techniques. One of these new methods was the *parejas*, or pair-trawling system, in which two large trawlers tow a huge net between them, in contrast to the usual method of one vessel towing one trawl. In a typical operation observed by Dr. W. R. Martin of the Fisheries Research Board of Canada, the 140-foot trawler *Playa de la Concha* fished with an identical twin, the *Elizodo*. The net towed between the two vessels was over three times as large as the otter trawl, with a head rope 320 feet long and a foot rope 390 feet long. Pieces of chain kept the foot rope on the bottom, and a continuous string of about 180 glass floats raised the head rope to give the net a tremendous mouth opening. On broad areas of smooth bottom the two vessels were as much as a half mile apart while towing. The net was towed for two to four hours, and typical catch was 6,000 pounds of fish, about two-thirds of it cod, the remainder of halibut, haddock, flounder, and skates was thrown back as unmarketable. The cod were dressed and split on deck and salted in the hold. Daily catches for a pair averaged about 20,000 pounds of fresh cod (which equals 6,000 pounds of salt cod) and about 10,000 pounds of discarded fish. Although the gear and methods of the *parejas* are impressive, the catches are about the same as for a single otter trawler of the same size as each of the pair-trawlers. Thus there seems to be little economic advantage in the pair-trawling system.

Nevertheless, the Spaniards spread their pair-trawling campaign for cod to the Nova Scotian banks and to fishing grounds off New England and New York. During reconnaissance flights with the U.S. Coast Guard, U.S. Bureau of Commercial Fisheries management agents observed ten Spanish pair-trawlers about twenty miles northwest of Corsair Canyon (about 150 miles east of Cape Cod) fishing for large cod. In addition, the Spanish fleets included a number of large stern trawlers on the Northeast Peak of Georges Bank. Fair catches of cod were observed on the decks of two of the vessels.

Spain's cod-fishing interests have also been extended to cooperative ventures with Latin American nations. A "super-trawler," originally named *Arcos* and built for a group of Spanish owners, was renamed *Mar Caribe* and outfitted for Cuba in the yards of the Vigo (Spain) Shipbuilding Consortium. This 315-foot vessel is one of the largest fishing vessels in the Cuban fleet. It is powered by a 4,000-horsepower diesel engine, is equipped with a fully automated processing factory, carries a crew of eighty-two men, and has enough room in the hold for about 2,000 metric tons of frozen fish. The traditional food of Cuba includes several dishes based on *bacalao*, most of which was imported from Norway and Newfoundland. The factory/freezer trawlers of the *Mar Caribe* class will permit Cuba to develop her own salt-fish industry.

In another venture, Spain is cooperating with a Mexican firm to supply *bacalao* to the Mexican market. The firm, Empresa Bacaladera Mexicana, S.A., was organized in Mexico with Spanish money. A processing plant was built near Mexico City to clean, cut, and finish drying the salt cod landed by two Spanish vessels fishing in the Northwest Atlantic. The first landing of 500 metric tons of *bacalao* produced under the joint agreement was distributed throughout Mexico just before the Christmas season, when it is in great demand for traditional holiday dishes. After the Christmas season, when Mexican demand slackens, the fish is exported to other Latin American countries, particularly in Central America.

Mexican officials are very much in favor of the venture because the quality of the product is considerably improved over the imported fish. Further, a saving of about 25 per cent is realized over the traditional price of thirty-five pesos per kilo (about $1.27 per pound).

The two Spanish vessels, which carried only Spanish fishermen on the first trip, sailed on the second voyage with five Mexicans in each crew. The vessels are now manned by all-Mexican crews.

While the cod fisheries mentioned earlier—both traditional or newly developed—are based on ancient cod stocks, that of Greenland is based on a new stock. Historically, the population of Greenland lived by hunting marine and land mammals. However, during the 1920's the sea off Greenland's west coast became warmer, and cod appeared in abundance. At the same time the seal herds left the area and the Greenlanders turned to fishing for cod, which they salted for export. Planners responsible for Greenland's future realized that ocean temperatures may once more decline, causing these stocks to decline or disappear. Cod in West Greenland waters are near the northern boundary of their range, and even small variations in water temperature can have great influence on the survival of the eggs and larvae. Dr. W. Dansgaard of the Copenhagen University Institute of Physics stated that Greenland's cod fisheries literally hinge on a 1.5-degree Centigrade rise or decline in the average annual ocean temperature off her west coast. He noted that a buildup of atmospheric carbon dioxide from air pollution may bring about a "greenhouse effect" to warm up the atmosphere by retaining the heat of the sun, and thus warm up the ocean. On the other hand, an increased load of particulate matter in the atmosphere (again, from air pollution) may act to screen out the sun's rays and thus cool the surface of the earth, including the oceans.

Danish fishery biologists, including Dr. Paul M. Hansen, one of the world's leading authorities on the cod, have kept careful records of the total number of cod caught from each year-class since 1924. The relative strength of each year-class has then been studied in relation to the temperature of the water lying above major cod-spawning areas off West Greenland. The relationship is not exact, but in general the warmer the mean temperature of the uppermost forty-five meter layer of water in these areas during June, the stronger has been the year-class of cod. For example, "rich" year-classes were produced in 1960 and 1961, "warm" years. The 1966 and 1967 year-classes, however, were very weak and resulted in a decline in the cod fishery; in 1968, it was a fifth to a third of what it had been the year before. These fluctuations are of considerable concern to the Greenland fishing industry, but the planners decided that cod must continue to be a major part of the developing economy despite the doubts about the permanence of the resource.

No great wisdom is needed to forecast the future of the world cod fishery. Its past history of fluctuations between scarcity and abundance undoubtedly will continue, perhaps with a general downward trend. The demand for cod probably will continue at about the same level because of the established eating habits of the cod-consuming nations, but the supply of cod may decline as a result of adverse changes in the environment from worldwide pollution of the ocean. Traces of DDT and other pesticides, for example, have been found in a variety of fishes, including marine species. The pesticide residues are deposited in the fatty tissues, and in the case of the cod and other "lean" fishes, the main sites are the liver and ovaries. DDT has been indicted as a cause of reproductive failure in birds and is thought to have a similar effect on fishes.

And now the cod may be threatened. In March 1971, the Swedish Department of Fisheries reported that considerable quantities of DDT were found in the ovaries of cod caught in the Baltic Sea. The levels were such that the Swedish authorities declared the ovaries (eaten in the Scandinavian countries) a health hazard and banned them from sale.

Mercury is another pollutant to be considered. Although it does not appear to be harmful to fish except in very high concentrations, mercury in the flesh could cause the fish to be removed from the market as unsafe for human consumption. The U.S. Food and Drug Administration (FDA) has set an upper limit of one-half part of mercury to a million parts of fish (0.5 ppm). Swordfish is banned from sale because it contains as much as 2.0 ppm of mercury. Jack Foehrenbach of my own Division of Marine and Coastal Resources and Dr. James Alexander of the N.Y. Ocean Science Laboratory recently completed an intensive survey of the mercury content of nearly a dozen marine species. Cod flesh was found to contain very low concentrations, averaging about 0.15 ppm.

The pollutants dumped into the ocean include sewage (both liquid and solid wastes), a host of chemicals, radioactive substances, and oil. All of these, together with natural changes in the environment, may result in a serious, long-term decline in cod abundance and availability, followed by a decline in the world fishery for cod.

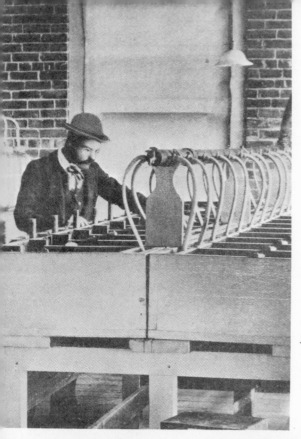

Cod hatcheries, such as this early one at Woods Hole, released millions of fry without discernible effect on sea populations. Below, U.S. and Soviet biologists aboard a Russian research trawler sort fish in a cooperative study off the New England-Middle Atlantic Coast. (National Marine Fisheries Service, Albert C. Jensen)

12

Conservation of the Cod

"BE CONTENT, the sea hath fish enough." Thus, in 1732, the British man of letters Dr. Thomas Fuller summed up an attitude toward marine resources that prevailed until the past half century. Modern fishery scientists don't agree with this philosophy but can understand the rationale behind it. If the herring fishery fails, we can fish for cod. And if the cod should leave, we can sail a few leagues farther to find them in abundance. Hadn't the explorers of the New World taken cod aplenty in baskets hoisted over the sides of their vessels? Even in the mid-nineteenth century, Dr. Thomas Huxley, the British biologist, wrote, "I believe that the cod fishery . . . and probably all the great sea fisheries are inexhaustible: that is to say, that nothing we do seriously affects the number of fish."

But the sea fisheries are not inexhaustible, and on both sides of the Atlantic Ocean the disquieting thought is being voiced that perhaps there is need to manage our sea fisheries, regulate the harvest, and help at least maintain the productivity of the sea.

Some thought *had* been given to the matter of conservation of sea fishes long before Fuller and Huxley made their sweeping—and quite erroneous—pronouncements. In sixteenth-century England, fishermen complained about mesh sizes in the crude trawl nets used by other fishermen in the Thames estuary, which, they argued, were capturing and killing all the small, unmarketable fish (a complaint that is repeated in other fisheries even in the twentieth century). So it was that in 1558,

Queen Elizabeth I published a Royal Decree setting a minimum limit of two and a half inches on the size of the mesh.

Trawl nets have always been looked on as mixed blessings. They are extremely efficient at catching large quantities of fish in a relatively short time. However, they catch fish of all sizes and the small, unmarketable ones are thrown back into the sea. These discarded fishes are either dead or dying by the time they are returned to the water and so are wasted for man's use. The great increase in British trawling in the late 1890's pointed up the wastefulness of small meshes and marked the beginning of serious research with nets to find a proper "savings gear." The ideal savings gear would have meshes large enough to allow the small unmarketable fish to escape but would retain all the marketable ones. Despite the early concern, however, it was not until 1934 that Great Britain formally passed a mesh regulation. And in 1936, the member nations of the International Council for the Exploration of the Sea (ICES) followed suit.

The specter of overfishing and the fear of what it would do to the resources were uppermost in the minds of far-thinking men even as Huxley was setting forth his optimistic statement. In 1860, the Norwegians began to keep careful records of the catches of cod landed at their northern fishing villages in the Lofoten Islands. By keeping track of the catches and of the number of fishing boats needed to make that catch, they could obtain an index of abundance—catch per vessel —that is still used today in scientific fishery management. In this way the fisheries scientists could determine if the abundance of the cod increased or decreased. Previously, there had been no way of knowing if increases and decreases in the total landings of cod reflected real changes in the number of cod in the sea. Furthermore, as more vessels fished the total catch of all the vessels would increase, giving the impression that there was an abundance of fish. When the catch per vessel was calculated, however, it might show that each trawler actually caught only a small volume of fish and that the true abundance was low.

The Lofoten cod fishery is a near-ideal study. There are no trees on the rocky Lofotens, which emerge from the sea off Norway's fjord-indented northwest coast, and Alplike peaks provide a towering backdrop to tiny fishing villages. Although the islands are at the same latitude as northern Alaska, the climate, like that of most of northern

Europe, is moderated by the North Atlantic Current, an extension of the warm Gulf Stream. This mighty ocean current flows north between Iceland and Britain and keeps the Lofoten ports ice-free and at the same time nurtures teeming schools of valuable fish. Between the islands and the mainland lies stormy Vestfjordan, fifty miles wide at the southern entrance and funneling northeastward to narrow, cliffbound straits. Into Vestfjorden every February flows a river of cod making their way to spawning grounds. Norsemen have been catching spawning cod in Vestfjorden since before there was written history in Norway. For at least a thousand years, they have exported dried codfish (*törrfisk*) and cod-liver oil caught off the Lofotens.

The pioneer in the scientific study of this far-northern population of cod was the Norwegian biologist G. O. Sars, who recognized the value of the resource and realized very early that information was needed as a basis for sound management and conservation of the fishery. He published the results of his studies in a definitive work, *Report of Practical and Scientific Investigations of the Cod Fisheries near the Loffoden* [sic] *Islands, Made during the Years 1864–1869*. Sars's report aroused a great deal of interest among scientists concerned with fisheries problems, especially in the newly established U.S. Commission of Fish and Fisheries. The report was translated into English and published in the Annual Report of the Commissioner in 1879. Sars wrote a similar report for the years 1870–73, and this too was translated and published by the Commission as a guide for U.S. studies on food fishes off the New England coast.

Sars was one of those rare prophets who is honored by his own country. As a sign of its appreciation for his work on the fish that means so much to Norway's economy, the government named a fisheries research vessel after him. The R/V *G. O. Sars* has made many important expeditions, especially on the northern seas inhabited by the Arctic cod. On one series of cruises she was used in a survey technique that is to fisheries studies what aerial photography is to forest-enumeration studies. She surveyed the waters between Bear Island and Spitzbergen with sensitive echo sounders in an effort to delimit the schools of cod and to relate them to hydrographic conditions. Three times she quickly moved across the chill waters while the echo sounders "searched" the waters with beams of sound. A fourth sweep was made slowly several weeks later. After the reams of paper echograms were studied and related to the bathythermograph temperature traces, the patterns of the cod schools were found. The cod always were bounded by a cold-water barrier.

Johan Hjort was another Norwegian who pioneered in studies on the cod. He too was concerned about the ups and downs in abundance and looked to ways to conserve the fish and insure its future availability on the tables of Europe. His findings were published in 1914 in a 228-page volume titled *Fluctuations in the Great Fisheries of Northern Europe*.

Hjort's 1911 studies included experiments in which he marked over a thousand cod with tags that consisted of silver buttons attached to the gill covers with silver wire. He found that cod tagged in the Vestfjord moved seasonally in response to their spawning urges. The experiment demonstrated that they move northward from the Lofoten Islands following their spring spawning and thus were no longer available to the island fishermen. Hjort also was able to show some of the effects of fishing on these cod stocks; between 15 per cent and 30 per cent of the tagged fish were caught by fishermen within one month after the tagging, which indicated that that proportion of the Vestfjord cod fell victim to the fishermen's nets with an additional—but unknown—percentage dying from "natural" causes. The causes for natural mortality include attacks by sharks, seals, and other predators, disease, accidents, and—rarely—old age.

The technology available to Hjort did not allow him to establish a definitive description of the total mortality of this group of cod, and he was not able to accurately describe the combination of fishing mortality and natural mortality that each year removed so many fish from the stock in the Westfjord area. Nevertheless, his work did provide a clue to suggest that some conservation measures would be needed. As with Sars, Johan Hjort was memorialized for his work with the launching of a Norwegian fisheries vessel, the R/V *Johan Hjort*.

Norwegian efforts to further the work begun by her pioneering fishery scientists went on under the able direction of Dr. Gunnar Rollefsen, for many years Director of the Havundersøkelser Fiskeridirektoratets in Bergen. His research on the cod, in the 1930's, provided additional background information on the life history of the species. Starting with studies on cod eggs and the environmental influences on them, Rollefsen moved on to studies of the artificial propagation of cod. This was almost a traditional approach based on the idea that if

Nature fails to provide adequate spawning, man can intercede to supplement the natural production with artificial production of young fish from hatcheries. Although hatcheries have been successful with freshwater fishes, especially the salmons and trouts, they have been dismal failures with most marine fishes. It is not surprising, then, that Rollefsen turned away from artificial propagation to research on the age and growth of the cod in Norwegian waters. Age and growth data provide the very foundation for fishery conservation regulations by helping fishery managers determine the optimum age at which fishermen can begin harvesting the species to insure that the young, immature individuals are allowed to mature and spawn at least once. The data help the gear specialist design the mesh size or hook size that will "select" the mature fish. And, with data from tagging experiments, physical characteristics of the same species from different fishing grounds, blood-type studies, and surveys of fish populations (such as echo-sounder surveys), age and growth data help determine the need for separate conservation regulations for various geographic areas.

Gunnar Rollefsen was aboard the R/V *Johan Hjort* during a survey cruise when he supplemented the diagrammatic trace from the echo sounder with a photograph taken by an underwater camera to precisely determine the presence of cod. Deep-water photography (and, following World War II, underwater television) offers obvious solutions to the question of just what species of fish make the echo-sounder traces. One of the technical difficulties Rollefsen faced was the problem of getting any kind of a recognizable picture with the camera twisting and turning at the end of a long cable attached to the ship, which itself was pitching and rolling. Off the Lofoten Islands, Rollefsen noticed persistent echoes from schools of fish twenty to thirty fathoms below. He lowered the camera into the gloom and made a series of exposures with artificial light. Some of the pictures only showed long streaks and bright, starlike spots, light reflections from the plankton, but others showed dim shapes, masses of fish frustratingly hazy in the gloomy depths. The prize photograph, however, showed a large, distinct, clearly recognizable cod directly in front of the camera lens.

The photographs, together with specimens of cod captured with nets set in those depths, left no doubt that the traces made by the echo sounder indeed represented aggregations of cod. This clearly demonstrated the value of using the echo sounder for making surveys of fish populations. Rollefsen's underwater photography also led the way for motion pictures and underwater television (UTV) to provide fishery scientists with an eye in the sea.

At about the same time the Norwegians were taking a serious look at the state of their fisheries, the British began to investigate their own fisheries. A Royal Commission on trawling began to collect statistics on catches and number of boats starting about 1885. These data were analyzed by Walter Garstang and published in 1900 in a report titled, "The Impoverishment of the Sea . . . Alleged Depletion of the Trawling Grounds." Garstang had looked at the conditions of the British fishing industry during a ten-year period when the steam trawler boom was at a height. He found that the total catch of all the vessels had increased by nearly one-third from 1889 to 1898. But during the same period the number of vessels had increased by two-and-a-half times while the actual catch per vessel had declined to about a half. In addition, the average size of the fish in the catch had decreased. If the trend were allowed to continue, he reasoned, the fleets soon would be harvesting many of the young fish before they had had an opportunity to spawn, which would ultimately result in serious depletion of the population, a real impoverishment of the sea.

Garstang's work was supplemented by another fisheries scientist, T. W. Fulton of the Scottish Fishery Board, who was one of the first men to describe experiments with savings gear. He used a twenty-five-foot beam trawl with a small-mesh cover over the cod-end. As the net was fished, small fish escaped from the cod-end by swimming through the meshes into the cover. A comparison on deck of the ship of the sizes of fish retained in the trawl and those that had escaped into the cover gave an index to the "size selection" of the mesh. As different nets with different-size meshes were tried, the biologist could determine the optimum mesh size for the species he wished to protect.

Another British fishery scientist, Ernest W. L. Holt, also was concerned about this wholesale destruction of immature cod and other fish caught by the trawlers. In 1895, he described his experiments in which he had used an otter trawl with a cod-end of square-mesh netting. He also tried a wooden frame and spreader poles in the cod-end in an effort to keep the meshes open to the maximum and thus make escape easy for the young cod, haddock, and other "round" fishes (as opposed to the flat fishes such as flounder). Holt reported that the rigid frame was quite effective in allowing the small fish to escape and the square-mesh netting worked well when new. However, as the netting softened with use, the meshes assumed more of a diamond shape, thus cutting down the escapement.

For his pioneering work in fisheries, Holt, like Sars and Hjort in Norway, was commemorated by having a fisheries vessel named after him. The R/V *Ernest Holt* was launched in 1949 to begin a distinguished career in fisheries-oceanographic research in the northern seas of Europe.

The ideas, speculations, and research of Sars, Hjort, Holt, and the others largely fell on deaf ears. After all, wasn't the sea inexhaustible? No less a personage than Professor T. H. Huxley had said so, and when one viewed puny man against the mighty seas, it seemed clear that Huxley must be right.

Basil Engholm, Fisheries Secretary of England and Wales, states, "There was an occasional voice preaching the opposite doctrine as early as the 1860's, notably Frank Buckland, whose views on the importance of allowing small fish to survive and grow to a worthwhile size were far in advance of his time. Gradually towards the end of the 19th century these views came to be held more widely, and some of the more far-sighted scientists, many fishermen, and some politicians began to be anxious at the decreasing size of catch for a given fishing effort."

It took the cataclysm of World War I to demonstrate that the conservationists were right and Huxley and his followers were wrong.

Prior to World War I, the scientists who advocated protection of fishes in the sea spoke largely on the basis of theory and conjecture. They could present no proof that the fish stocks were in a state of decline as a result of fishing effort, at least no proof that the average fisherman would accept. Thus, in the opinion of the industry, there was no need to regulate the fishing effort to conserve the fish stocks. However, the severe restriction on fishing in the period 1913–18, the result of wartime shortages of fishermen, gear, and supplies, plus the menace of submarines prowling on the fishing grounds, provided the proof the scientists needed. During nearly five years of greatly reduced fishing effort, the stocks of fish had been able to survive and grow unmolested by man. Basil Engholm says that "in 1919 the average landing per day's absence of an English trawler from the North Sea was 30.6 cwts [3060 pounds] compared with 14.3 cwts [1430 pounds] in 1913."

The fishing hiatus during the war had allowed the fish to grow bigger and heavier instead of being caught in the trawls, and no small fish were tossed overboard as so much waste. It was not that there were twice as many fish as before but that the fish on the grounds had been able to grow and increase in weight.

But the lesson that might have been learned from this gigantic demonstration of fish saving quickly went by the board. The fish stocks that had benefited by the wartime reduction of fishing effort soon were heavily exploited as before. Any man who could raise the price of a trawler and recruit a crew was on the grounds to take advantage of the large catches. This short-sighted attitude to make an immediate profit with little regard for the future of the stocks soon reduced the fish to their prewar level, or even lower. The fisheries biologists tried to make the industry and the government fisheries officers see what was happening, but no administrative action was taken.

The lesson, however, did stimulate the scientists, who now had practical proof of their theories. The years between the two world wars was a time of advances in the study of the dynamics of fisheries and in the formulation of scientific ideas of fish conservation.

On the western side of the North Atlantic, North Americans too were voicing a concern about the cod and other sea fishes. They had started in an earlier time, when the fishing banks of the New World were still thought of as the Eldorado of cod. A protective measure was enacted in 1639 by the General Court of the Massachusetts Bay colony, which ordered that no cod were to be used as fertilizer for farm crops.

There were no restrictions on fishing, however, and as the abundance declined in the local waters the New Englanders went farther and farther offshore in their quest for cod.

Few people seemed worried about the continued supply of cod off the northeast coast of the American continent. Perhaps it was too incredible to even imagine that the great populations on Georges Bank or on the Grand Bank could ever be affected by man's efforts. But there were discouraging changes in the abundance of cod, and a few perceptive observers suggested that all was not well. One of these was Spencer F. Baird.

Dr. Baird was a zoologist and naturalist who served as Assistant Secretary of the Smithsonian Institution in Washington. In 1871, President Ulysses S. Grant signed into law a resolution "for the protection and preservation of the food fishes of the coasts of the United States." He also appointed Baird as Commissioner of the newly created U.S. Fish

Commission, charged with the responsibility for conservation of the aquatic resources which appeared to be declining under intensive exploitation. Grant's action and the appointment of Baird had come about as the result of grumblings among New England fishermen. Shortly after the Civil War it was thought that the fisheries of Massachusetts and Rhode Island were declining because, as the fishermen complained, pound nets and traps along the coast were overfishing the stocks. But studies made by the two states contradicted each other. The fishermen appealed to Washington, and the federal government responded by setting up a research program at Woods Hole, Massachusetts, headed by Baird.

Baird's studies convinced him that fishing plus natural causes were causing the scarcity of fish, and he concluded that the pound nets were directly responsible and should be regulated. (Dr. J. L. McHugh of the Marine Sciences Research Center at Stony Brook says, "From our present vantage point, it appears very unlikely that the resources were being overfished.") But Baird was correct in concluding that both manmade and natural forces were at work.

The early studies of the Fish Commission concerned inshore fishes that then were the mainstay of the trap and pound-net fishermen— scup (*Stenotomus chrysops*), tautog (*Tautoga onitis*), and sea bass (*Centropristes striatus*). Later, they turned their attention to the cod fisheries and in 1874, Baird published his "Conclusions as to Decrease of Cod-Fisheries on the New England Coast." The decline, Baird wrote, is the result of man's activities. Dams built to help power New England textile mills blocked the spawning runs of alewives (*Alosa pseudoharengus*), an anadromous fish of the herring family that lives in the sea but ascends freshwater streams to lay its eggs. When alewife abundance declined, cod abundance also declined, and Baird linked the two events as cause and effect. Herring was the cod fishermen's bait, hence it must be an important cod food. (We know today, of course, that fishes form only a small part of the diet of cod; they feed mostly on invertebrates.) He was correct in fixing the blame for the scarcity of alewives, but wrong about the cod.

With Baird's report as a base, the Fish Commission soon embarked on an ambitious program to increase the number of cod in the sea and thus, they hoped, restore the fisheries to their former productivity. European fishery scientists had shown that the populations of fishes in streams and ponds could be enhanced, or at least maintained, by stocking fish raised in hatcheries. "Inference was made," says Dr. Paul S. Galtsoff in his history of the Woods Hole laboratory, "that by means of artificial propagation it would be possible to increase the supply of such fish as cod, flounder, shad, mackerel, halibut and other species, and also to transport them to other localities where they were not present."

Cod were first artificially hatched at Gloucester during the winter of 1878–79. Hatcheries also were built in Boothbay Harbor, Maine, and Woods Hole. John J. Brice, U.S. Commissioner of Fish and Fisheries, reported in 1898 that the "cod is propagated artificially on a more extensive scale than any other marine fish." Up to the season of 1896–97, a total of nearly 450 million cod fry had been liberated from the hatcheries. During the 1896–97 season a total of 98 million fry were liberated. Brice proclaimed the success of the hatchery operation and said, "The unmistakable economic results which have attended these efforts warrant all the time and money devoted to them and justify the greatest possible expansion of the work."

In addition to the shoreside facilities, the government launched the *Fish Hawk* as a floating hatchery. A German report of the time describes the vessel as a large steamship "with hundreds of large pieces of apparatus for hatching fish eggs. The steam engine partly serves for pumping of water and partly for moving to and fro in the water the apparatus attached to the sides of the vessel, thus vivifying the germs of the eggs." Fish Commission workers also accompanied commercial fishing vessels during the cod-spawning season to collect and fertilize the eggs of fish caught at sea. The work was done on board the vessels, and then the fertilized eggs were returned to the sea to develop and grow. Brice says that the spawntakers were given the run of the fishing vessel but were required to reimburse the captain twenty-five cents for each meal taken aboard.

Healthy, lively cod taken in fish traps or on vessels fishing in the inshore waters were taken to the Woods Hole hatchery to serve as brood fish. They were kept in floating live cars in a large outdoor pool, and as many as 1,600 to 9,000 fish were penned each season to insure a steady supply of eggs and sperm. The fish were removed periodically and examined to determine their stage of ripeness. If they were ripe, the eggs and sperm were stripped from the fish into containers with seawater and the contents stirred to obtain optimum fertilization. The fertilized eggs then were transferred to hatching trays for subsequent development. The newly hatched fry were taken from the trays and released in nearby waters, in the harbor at Gloucester and in Eel Pond at Woods Hole. It was at this stage that the entire hatchery scheme failed in its intended purpose.

The fry were released at a very early stage of development because they are difficult to rear to large size. Supplying adequate food of the right size and kind is perhaps the biggest obstacle. Under natural conditions a female cod may lay 4 million eggs, of which only a few will survive and grow to adulthood. The death rate is astronomical, and most young fish die in the early stages, perhaps in the first three months. Thus the hatchery fish were being released when they would be exposed to the greatest mortality. Despite the great faith that Brice and others had in the supposed benefit of hatcheries for marine fish, the fish that were stocked really added little if anything to the populations in the sea.

The methodology and techniques to measure or even determine this mortality were not available to these early hatchery workers, and so the rearing of fishes continued as a major work of the Bureau of Fisheries. In 1936, the Bureau reported:

The propagation of the commercial marine varieties of the North Atlantic coast has been carried on this year on a greatly enlarged scale in comparison with the last 2 or 3 years. While the Woods Hole, Mass. station has handled no cod, it has collected and hatched approximately 443,000,000 winter flounder eggs and is now working on mackerels.

At Boothbay Harbor, Maine, the season's operations have involved the handling of 1,128,000 flounder eggs, 648,000,000 cod eggs, and 101,000,000 haddock eggs.

The Gloucester, Mass. station is carrying on its offshore operations wherein spawntakers aboard the commercial fishing vessels take, fertilize, and plant overboard immediately such ripe eggs as are obtainable. Almost half billion pollock, 217,000,000 cod, 19,000,000 flatfish, and 9,000,000 haddock eggs have been checked in by this station. This work has been augmented in response to the desire of the fishing industry for more attention to what is literally a byproduct recovery.

At Woods Hole, the hatchery continued to function until the buildings were taken over by the U.S. Navy in World War II. It had ended somewhat earlier at Gloucester and Boothbay Harbor.

In the early 1930's, the research emphasis of the Woods Hole laboratory took on a more modern direction. Some of the basic biological studies of growth, physiology, behavior, and embryology continued —as did the hatchery work—but some of the newer aspects of fisheries science were launched. The American biologists, like their European colleagues, realized that to conserve the cod and other fishery stocks it was necessary to first gain an understanding of the dynamics of the populations. Information was needed about age and growth, fishing mortality and natural mortality, spawning characteristics, migration and other movements of the fish, and the presence of separate populations of a species. The workers at the laboratory turned to a statistical approach for some of the information. Data were collected from the commercial landings including analyses of the catches, length measurements of representative samples of fish in the catch, and collections of scales and otoliths for age determination.

Conservation of the resource had to be based on good management and good management had to be based on a thorough knowledge of the stocks. Much of the information could be gained by marking fish with tags and observing the details of their recapture weeks, months, or even years later. Cod had been tagged in the northeast Atlantic at least as early as 1888, but it was not until 1897 that any were marked on the American side, and that initial four-year experiment produced few returns, apparently because many of the copper tags dropped off the fish. A monumental tagging experiment at sea took place from 1923 to 1929 in New England waters when William C. Schroeder of the U.S. Bureau of Fish released nearly 25,000 cod with tags attached. A few years later, from 1926 to 1940, Canadian biologists tagged and released about 20,000 cod in the waters off Nova Scotia, in the Gulf of St. Lawrence, and on the offshore banks. Both the U.S. and Canadian studies were stimulated by the newly formed North American Council on Fishery Investigations (NACFI).

The results of the many tagging experiments in European and North American waters clearly demonstrated that there is no interchange between the cod of the northeast Atlantic and those of the northwest Atlantic. They further showed that there are several separate ecological groups of fish. For example, Grand Bank fish are separate from Nova Scotian fish; Georges Bank fish are separate from the southern New

England fish, and so on. Similar groups exist in European waters. There are, of course, a few fish that move from one group to another, but generally they are considered separate for management purposes.

Although a number of fishery biologists advocated that some management be instituted to conserve the stocks, little actually was done. The specter of overfishing and destruction of immature fish by the otter trawl was very much part of the scene. American biologists paid almost as much attention to the devastation of fish by the otter trawl as their European colleagues had, but the problem showed up later on the western side of the Atlantic because the trawl was introduced later there. In 1912, seven years after the otter trawl was introduced to American waters, the Massachusetts Commission on Fisheries and Game completed an investigation of steam trawling to learn what damage might be done to the fisheries by the gear. Fishermen who were still fishing with hooks and lines from dories vigorously opposed the trawl, and many of them banded together to petition state legislators to prohibit, or at least restrict, this new fishing method. Indeed, their complaints were valid. The hooks took only large, mature fish, and any immature fish they happened to take were quickly returned alive to the water. In contrast, the otter trawl was indiscriminate in its catches.

The Massachusetts trawling study was made on Georges Bank aboard the *Foam*, a 126-foot steel trawler. David L. Belding, biologist in charge of the study, reported that 25 per cent of the haddock they caught were too small for market and were discarded at sea. The cod they caught were larger, only 14.3 per cent of them had to be discarded. He concluded that "the mortality among the fish thrown overboard is probably about . . . 100 per cent for small haddock and cod."

As a result of Belding's report, the U.S. Bureau of Fisheries undertook a more elaborate investigation of the effects of otter trawling. This study corroborated the results of the earlier study and, in fact, showed that the damage was more serious. The investigators found that the destruction of immature fish, by weight, was 40 per cent for cod and 38 per cent for haddock during June to December, but only 3 per cent for cod and 11 per cent for haddock during January to May. The seasonal differences represent the abundance of small, young-of-the-year fish of both species during the latter half of the year. The congressional committee that received the report in 1915 recommended that otter trawling be restricted to certain banks and that the fish populations be monitored in subsequent years to determine the effect trawling might have on the abundance of cod and haddock. The committee also warned, "We emphatically state it to be our opinion that this regulation will prove futile and an unnecessary imposition on American fishermen unless Canada, particularly, and possibly Newfoundland and France will take such action as will prevent or restrict the use of the trawl on the banks in the western North Atlantic." As Dr. William C. Herrington said later, "The [fishing] industry did not see fit to support these recommendations; consequently, at that time, neither the United States nor other Governments took further action."

The dramatic rise in fish landings following World War I and II was not nearly so evident in the North American fisheries as it had been in Europe. In the New England cod fishery, for example, landings were 45.4 million pounds in 1913, and 51.2 million pounds in 1920. In 1939 landings were 50.6 million pounds, and 43.1 million pounds in 1947. It is possible that there had been some benefit from the reduced fishing effort during the war years but it could not be demonstrated for the cod. Further, the interest of U.S. fishery biologists in the years between the two wars was diverted from cod to haddock and this fishery was having many of its own problems. Following World War II, however, the creation of the International Commission for the Northwest Atlantic Fisheries (ICNAF) again focused attention on the cod fishery.

International commissions have been established in many parts of the world for the management and conservation of aquatic resources. Most of them have had mediocre success, particularly with regard to fisheries, and have served primarily as forums for discussion and debate. Certainly this is true of the Atlantic commissions. Their principal success has been in conducting research and gathering data for the scientific advisors to present to the commissioners. But the commissioners, because of their nationalistic and political leanings, in too many cases choose to ignore the recommendations of their advisors.

The oldest such body in the Atlantic is the International Council for the Exploration of the Seas (ICES). In 1899, inspired by the statements of Buckland, Garstang, Hjort, and others, the Swedish government invited interested countries to a conference in Stockholm, the outcome of which was the formation of ICES in 1902. The founding member nations were Denmark, Finland, Germany, Holland, Norway, Russia, Sweden, and the United Kingdom. The membership today also includes France, Belgium, Italy, Spain, Portugal, Iceland, and Ireland.

Three working committees were established, on fish migration, on overfishing, and on the biology of the Baltic Sea. ICES promoted the launching of international surveys of the distribution of fish stocks in the North Sea, the distribution of plankton (the primary producers of the sea), and surveys of the hydrography of the sea.

The surveys provided much of the groundwork for national research on fish stocks and for conservation measures that were to follow in later years. One such measure was developed during international conferences in London in November 1936 and March 1937. The objective of the conferences was to agree on a uniform mesh size for the northeast Atlantic and to set minimum sizes for the most important species of white fish (cod, haddock, hake, etc.). Although an agreement was drawn up, it was never ratified because of the outbreak of the war in 1939. Following the war, however, a conference was held that, in 1954, set a minimum mesh size limit of 75mm (3 inches), with 110mm for Arctic and Icelandic waters because cod and haddock tend to be larger there. The member nations also were required to establish minimum sizes at which cod, haddock, hake, and flatfishes could be landed and sold. These conservation measures were expanded with the drawing up of the Northeast Atlantic Fisheries Convention (NEAFC) in 1959. Additional measures set restrictions on type of gear, closed seasons and areas, and regulation of fishing effort or the amount of the total catch. Harking back to the early days of fishery biology, the NEAFC member nations were to improve and increase marine resources "which may include artificial propagation, the transplantation of organisms, and the transplantation of young."

In the northwest Atlantic, the earliest international commission was NACFI, whose membership included France, Canada, and the United States. The council existed from 1920 to 1938 and its prime accomplishment was the setting up of a statistical system for the collection of information on the catches and activities of the members operating in the council area. The fishing grounds off Canada's Maritimes, Newfoundland, and New England were divided into a number of statistical areas based largely on natural ecological divisions and what was known of the fish populations in each area. These areas were then further subdivided on the basis of refinements of the ecological criteria, especially depth. Thus it was possible to pinpoint the location of a particular catch within an area as small as ten by fifteen nautical miles, which enabled the fishery biologist to compare the age structure, size composition, or relative abundance of fish from, for example, the southwest part of Georges Bank and the northern edge of Georges Bank.

Although NACFI achieved little else, its statistical areas did serve as the basis for that of ICNAF, which held its first meeting in 1951. ICNAF was established for the "investigation, protection and conservation of the fisheries of the Northwest Atlantic Ocean, in order to make possible the maintenance of a maximum sustained catch from those fisheries." The area covered by the convention included the entire northwest Atlantic from the west coast of Greenland, Labrador, Newfoundland, and Nova Scotia, to New England as far south as Rhode Island. Twelve nations, including the United States and Canada, signed the convention. Most of them were concerned with the rich cod fisheries on the Grand Banks, in the Gulf of St. Lawrence, and on the Scotian Shelf. As with its northeast Atlantic counterparts, ICNAF was early concerned with savings-gear experiments to reduce the destruction of young fish in otter trawls.

In the United States the experiments were centered on the haddock, while in Canada and other member nations they were centered on the cod. I took part in many of the mesh experiments at sea in which teams of biologists and technicians measured hundreds of thousands of fish. In addition, we crawled inside the trawls on deck before and after they had been fished, and measured thousands of meshes to relate the sizes of mesh to the sizes of fish. Later, with scuba, I rode the trawls as they were towed on the bottom to study the configuration of the meshes and of the entire nets. Underwater television was also used for prolonged study or in water too deep for divers.

The experiments uncovered differences between species in their escapement through the meshes. For example, more cod of all sizes escape than haddock. More than anything, this showed that regulating mesh sizes as a conservation measure is not nearly as simple as many biologists would like to believe. Nevertheless the U.S. government produced legislation in 1953 that established four and a half inches (114mm) as the minimum mesh size for the haddock fishery on the New England banks, replacing the former two and a quarter inches. The rest of ICNAF followed suit, and today minimum mesh sizes are five and one-eighth inches (130mm) for West Greenland waters and four and a half inches in the remainder of the convention area. Scientists of the member nations also examined the possible destruction of small fish caught by gill nets, traps, and hooks, and found that none of these was as destructive as the otter trawl.

How effective is mesh regulation as a conservation measure? Not very, it seems. In the case of haddock, Dr. Herbert W. Graham, former Director of the Woods Hole fisheries laboratory, says that changes in numbers of catchable fish and in levels of fishing effort make it impossible to determine the actual effects of mesh regulation; the benefits, he points out, "simply have to be taken as an article of faith." This is very reminiscent of the attitude of the fish culturists who tried to replenish stocks in the sea with artificially propagated fry. No benefit from stocking could be demonstrated scientifically, but the culturists couldn't help believing that their efforts were doing some good, and this faith sustained their programs for many years. Today, some experts in the dynamics of fish populations contend that mesh regulation for such species as cod and haddock is just as ineffective as artificial propagation—and for much the same reasons: Natural phenomena and man's other fishing activities are too powerful as depleting factors.

This certainly seems to be true in the cod fishery. Because of the great number of vessels operating, overfishing has reduced the cod populations on many grounds. Further, as the abundance of other species declined, the fishery for cod has increased to satisfy consumer demand, as is happening today in the New England fishery. The New England offshore fleet traditionally sought haddock, but with the collapse of this fishery, the fleet turned to cod. Fortunately, in recent years there have been a series of successful spawnings so that the cod population on Georges Bank and other nearby grounds is in relatively good condition. At this moment, the New England stocks of cod are being assessed by Woods Hole biologists to determine if they are in a state of decline or increase and to see if they can support the present level of effort. We need only look to other grounds to see how precarious the local cod populations are and on what relatively minor factors they depend.

Off Greenland, cod are present because of a 1.5 degree Centigrade change in average annual sea temperature. In Norwegian waters, there was very poor spawning in 1965 and 1966. The reason for the failures is not known but, according to the Norwegian fisheries periodical *Fiskaren*, it is assumed that some catastrophe occurred during the spawning season. As a result, there was poor fishing for small cod in 1969 and

[171]

1970, and Norwegian scientists predicted poor fishing for large cod in 1973 and 1974. In the Barents Sea, low abundance of capelin, a favorite cod food, resulted in low abundance and small catches of cod. In Danish waters, large numbers of dead cod were seen among other dead and dying fish, birds, and marine invertebrates following an outbreak in October 1968 of "red tide" (*Gymnodinium breve*). The fish were killed by the toxin produced by this planktonic dinoflagellate. Natural disasters such as these very easily diminish the effect of conservation measures such as mesh regulations.

There is little we can do about natural mortality, and mesh regulation alone is almost like patching up one hole in a sieve. What is needed is a comprehensive conservation program. An approach to the solution of the overfishing problem, at least for the Barents Sea, was voiced by Hallstein Rasmussen, at a meeting of NEAFC in 1969:

> Rapidly diminishing resources of fish, particularly cod and related species, is one big problem for which a solution has yet to be found. . . . Conservation and replenishment of Northeast Atlantic fish resources depends on much more comprehensive measure than those considered up till now. . . . Nations fishing in the Barents Sea should reduce their total catch from its current level of 400,000 metric tons annually to 250,000 tons. . . . The best solution is to put a complete ban on trawling, at least in areas which are known as feeding grounds for fish before they reach maturity.

It is becoming increasingly evident that stern measures such as these must be taken to conserve the stocks of cod. The report of the NEAFC annual meeting in 1968 noted that "control of mesh sizes and minimum fish size had not been sufficient to obtain maximum sustainable yield, and therefore it seemed that effort control was necessary." The question of which nations shall fish, with how many vessels, and for how long a time, is still being debated. At the conclusion of the meeting, it was decided that the problem should be studied and a report presented to the commission at its next meeting.

There is the danger, however, that we may study the problem of overfishing the cod to the near extinction of the species. We have seen this happen with the Georges Bank haddock, which has been intensively studied for nearly forty years. Herbert W. Graham says this stock "is the most thoroughly understood in the Convention Area and probably one of the best known in the world." Today it is in dangerously low abundance.

In the United States, research on the cod resource is a matter of supervised neglect. While at one time it was the subject of many intensive biological studies, especially by government scientists, at the present little or no research is being carried on. During the latter part of the nineteenth century, most of the efforts were concerned with spawning studies and hatchery rearing. Later research concentrated on food habits, age and growth, and migrations and distribution. For about twenty-five years (from the early 1930's) little or no research was undertaken, but tagging and age-and-growth studies were reactivated and continued for about ten years (until about 1964). At the present time, data on lengths and numbers of fish caught are collected from the commercial fishery and from survey cruises. But to all intents and purposes, there is no U.S. research underway on the cod today.

The fishery scientists have shown the way. What is needed now to truly conserve the cod and other marine fishery resources are commissioners, administrators, and politicians who will forgo nationalistic prejudices and implement the management proposals.

Selected Bibliography

THE CLASSIC STORY OF codfishing was written by Rudyard Kipling, *Captains Courageous*, New York, Bantam Books. This novel is extremely factual in the descriptions of fishing gear and methods and of life aboard a nineteenth-century Gloucester dory schooner. Alan Villiers, *The Quest of the Schooner Argus*, New York, Charles Scribner's Sons, 1951, describes the modern-day Portuguese dory fishery for cod on the Grand Bank. James B. Connolly, *The Book of the Gloucester Fishermen*, New York, John Day Company, 1927, contains a wealth of anecdotes about the men and their lives aboard fishing vessels out of that famed New England port.

Abundant information on the history of European sea fisheries may be found in C. L. Cutting, *Fish Saving*, London, Leonard Hill (Books), 1955. D. H. Cushing, *The Arctic Cod*, London, Pergamon Press, 1966, deals with the modern European otter trawl fishery for cod and some of the research on the species. The role of marine fishes, including the cod, in providing food for man is given by C. P. Idyll, *The Sea Against Hunger*, New York, Thomas Y. Crowell Company, 1970. Georg Borgstrom and Arthur J. Heighway, *Atlantic Ocean Fisheries*, London, Fishing News (Books), 1961, describes the great effort expended by many of the nations that fish for cod in the North Atlantic. The origin and development of America's fishing industry in the northwest Atlantic may be found in Albert C. Jensen, *A Brief History of the New England Offshore Fisheries*, Washington, U.S. Bureau of Commercial Fisheries, 1967.

A good account of early explorations in the Northwest Atlantic is Julius E. Olson, *The Northmen, Columbus and Cabot*, New York, Charles Scribner's Sons, 1906. Farley Mowat, *Westviking, the Ancient Norse in Greenland and North America*, Boston, Little, Brown and Company, 1965, details the Viking contribution to early knowledge about northeastern North America and the coastal seas. A generalized account of the North Atlantic and the men who sailed it is Alan Villiers, *Wild Ocean*, New York, McGraw-Hill Book Company, 1957. Daniel P. Mannix, *Black Cargoes*, New York, Viking Press, 1965, deals with the Atlantic slave trade and the part played by the Yankee traders.

Index

Adams, J. G. B., 13
Adams, John, 109-111
Africa, demand for salt cod in, 63, 147
Alaska, cod and the acquisition of, 40-43
Albatross III, 44
Albatross IV, 137
Alert, 40
alewives, 28, 163
Alexander, James, 152
American Fisheries Society, 37
Anadyr, Gulf of, 43
anchoveta, 50
Anderson, Andrew W., 60
Andrea Doria, 47, 139
Anglo Saxon, 29
Ann, 106
Archer, Gabriel, 86
Arcos, 150
Arlington, 134
Antarctic fishery, 49-50, 75-76
auk, great, extinction of, 1, 6-7

Babson, John J., 90
Baird, Spencer F., 124, 162-163
Baltic Sea fishery, 143, 152
Barents Sea fishery, 4, 33, 143, 148, 172
Bay State, 134
Bay State Fishing Company, 128
Bear Island cod, 33, 34
Beaumont, William, 60
Behan, Les, 139
Belding, David L., 130, 167
Belis, Fannie, 30
Bell, Frederick W., 10-11
Bering Sea fishery, 40
Bielevich, Alphonse, 30-31, 140
Bigelow, Henry B., 48
Biscay, Bay of, 4

Birdseye, Clarence, 135
Blackburn, Howard, 122-123
Bluenose, 74
Bökönyi, Sándor, 51
Boothbay Harbor (Maine), hatchery at, 164, 165
Boston, (Mass.), 90
    trawler fleet of, 131
Boucicault, Dion, 12
Bourne, Edward G., 84
Brereton, John, 86
Brice, John J., 164
Brielle (N. J.), 140
brittle stars, 27
Brookes, 99
Browns Bank, 86
Buckland, Frank, 161
bultow, *see* line trawl
burbot, subspecies of, 48
Burgeo Bank, 122

Cabot, John, 83-85
Cabot, Sebastian, 83-85
Cacace, John, 141
Campanha Bachaloeira, 148
Campbell, Edgar O., 40
Canada:
    Atlantic Salt Fish Commission of, 107
    cod fishery of, 40
    Fisheries Research Board of, 43, 149
    St. Andrews Biological Station, 35
Cape Cod, 86, 121
    Canal, 51
Cape Breton Island fishery, 68, 84
capelin, 28, 148, 172
Capont, Francisco Lopez, 63
Captains Courageous (Kipling), 8, 117-120

Carmen, Charles, Jr., 139
Cashes Ledge, 90
Central America, demand for salt cod in, 63
Chaleur, Bay of, 112
Chance Cove, 29
Charles River, 49
Chesla, Joseph, 140
coal fish, see pollock
Cobb, John N., 40, 43
cod (see also cod, varieties of; cod fishery)
  bait for, 6-7, 28, 148
  as "beef of the sea," 5, 56-65
  cannibalism of, 27
  changes in harvesting of, 127-138
  conservation of, 155-173
  demand for, 2-3, 70, 72, 152
  description of, 4
  and discovery of America, 81-92
  dried salt, 5, 53, 55-56, 63, 68-70, 111, 113, 114
  estimating age of, 31-32
  in folk literature, 17-18
  food of, 27-29
  as food for slaves, 93
  and foreign fishing fleets, 137-138
  fresh, 135, 144
  eggs, 23-25, 165
  growth rate of, 29-30, 32
  habitat of, 4, 26-27
  larval, 25-26
  in poems, 14-17
  relationship between, and red jelly-fish, 25-26
  relationship between, and religion, 1, 5, 9-11, 18-19, 54, 55, 65, 144
  markets for, 63-65
  meaning of, as old-time word, 1, 11-12
  in Massachusetts House of Representatives, 12-13
  migration of, 33-36
  naming of the, 1-2
  nutritive value of, 60-61
  overfishing of, 137-138, 143, 167, 171-172
  populations of, 137-138
  and pollution of the ocean, 152-153
  record size of, 30-31
  and settlement of New England, 86-91

cod (cont.)
  spawning of, 4, 21-23, 33-35, 125, 137, 157, 171, 173
  and sport fishermen, 3, 30-31, 126, 138-141
  tagging of, 32-36 passim, 158, 166, 173
  traps, 61-62
cod, varieties of:
  Arctic, 43-44
  Atlantic, subspecies of, 37-43
  Baltic, 39
  black, see sablefish
  blue, 49
  bull, see cod, blue
  channel, 49
  cultus, see lingcod
  false, 49-50
  gray, see Pacific
  green, see pollock
  Greenland, 39
  Kildin Island, 39
  Pacific, 39-43 passim
  polar, 44
  poor, 47
  rock, 49
  saffron, 37
  toothed, 37
  White Sea, 39
  White Sea winter, 39
cod bangers, 71
cod fishery:
  development of domestic, 5-6
  development of world, 67-79
  economic importance of regional, 144-152 passim
  effects of technological advances on, 127-129, 134-135
  landings of world, 2, 30-31, 40, 43, 44, 49, 50, 65, 101, 134, 137, 143, 148, 168
  use of gill nets in, 124-125
  use of line trawl in, 124
cod-liver oil, 50, 54, 57-59
cod-rum-slave trade, 93-107
Company of Laconia, 88-89
Concord, 86
consumer preferences, changing, 135-137
Cooper, James Fenimore, 12
copers, 73
Corsair Canyon, 150

Cowley, Malcolm, 100, 103
Cox Ledge, 139
crabs, 27
Cross, Peter, 102
Cuba, cod fishery of, 138, 150
cusk, 37
Cutting, C. L., 53, 55, 89

Dannevig, G. M., 22
Dansgaard, W., 151
Denmark, distant-water trawlers
    from, 33
DDT, effect of, on fish, 152
dogfish, spiny, 27
Dogger Bank fishery, 71
dories, 74, 108, 112, 116-124, 148, 167
Drummond, J. C., 58
Duggan, James J., 140
Dunbar, M. J., 44
Durivage, Francis A., 12

East German fishery, 137-138, 144-146
echo sounder, use of, 159
Economics and Social History of
    New England (Weeden), 103
Eddie, Gordon, 78
Eddom, Harry, 76-77, 78
Edholm, Otto, 77
Eldey Island, 7
Elizabeth Islands, 87
Elizodo, 149
Empresa Bacaladera Mexicana, S.A.,
    150
Engholm, Basil, 161
Epaves Bay, 82
Ericson, Leif, 82
Ericson, Thorstein, 82
Ericson, Thorvald, 82
Ernest Holt, 161
Eskimos, 40, 43
Evermann, Barton W., 43

Faneuil, Peter, 104
Faroe Islands, 4
finnan haddie, 47
fish:
    conservation programs, 25
    consumption of, 54, 55, 62-63, 65
    destruction of immature, 167-168,
        170
    hatcheries, 22, 154, 164-166, 173
    minimum catch sizes of, 169

fish (cont.)
    population studies, 156-160, 172
    relationship between, and religion,
        1, 5, 9-11, 18-19, 144
    tagging of, 158, 166, 173
    using of, for industrial fish, oil,
        and meal, 50
fishermen:
    and change from hook-and-line
        fishing to trawling, 73
    dory, 74, 108, 112, 116-124, 148, 167
    "gray terror" of, x, 112, 121
    and fleeting, 72-73
    hand line, 67
    sport, 3, 30-31, 126, 138-141
    superstitions of, 77-78, 133
    the trawlermen as, 127-138 passim
    working life of, 4, 6, 74-76, 116-123
        passim, 129-130
Fishes of North and Middle America,
    The (Jordan and Evermann), 43
Fish Hawk, 164
fishing (see also fishermen)
    methods of, 28, 71, 113, 116-125
    winter, 121-123
fishing community and sea disasters,
    112
fishing gear, revolution in, 124-125
fish protein concentrate (FPC), 47-48
fish species, see names of fish
Fiskaren, 172
flatfish, 165, 169
flounder, 2, 51, 137, 149, 160
    yellowtail, 46
    winter, 165
Fluctuations in the Great Fisheries of
    Northern Europe (Hjort), 158
Foam, 167
Foehrenbach, Jack, 152
Fox, Charles, 58
FPC, see fish protein concentrate
France, cod fishery of, 4, 90, 138, 144,
    149
Fraser, Melville J., 130, 133
Fuller, Thomas, 155
Fulton, T. Wemyss, 160

Gadidae, 4, 37-39
Gallivan, James A., 13
Galtsoff, Paul S., 164
Garstang, Walter, 160
gastropods, 27

Georges Bank:
  cod fishery on, 4, 6, 86, 90-91
  haddock fishery on, 46, 135
  hake fishery on, 46
Gertrude L. Thebaud, x
Gloucester (Mass.), x, 6, 30, 90-91, 135
  Fishermen's and Seamen's Widows
    and Orphans Aid Society, 112
  fish hatchery at, 164-166
Golden Eagle, 74
Golden Triangle, The, 63, 93-104, 105-
  106
  collapse of, 104-107
Goode, G. B., 30, 101, 102
G. O. Sars, 157
Gosnold, Bartholomew, 5, 86-87
Grace L. Fears, 123
Graham, Herbert W., 171, 172-173
Graham, Michael, 26-27
Grand Bank:
  cod fishery on, 4, 30, 32, 35, 67, 81-
    85, 112, 143, 144
  and shipping lanes cross over, 28
  summer fog on, 121
Great Britain:
  Act of 1799 of, 69
  cod fishery of, 4, 33, 138
  domination of the seas by, 67
  fishermen of, 54-55, 90
  fishery rights in treaty between,
    and the U.S., 109-111
  fishery studies by, 160-161
  Medical Research council of, 77
  Molasses Act of, 104-105
  per capita fish consumption of, 65
  Royal Navy Mission to Deep Sea
    Fishermen, 73
  Sugar Act of, 105
  Truck Act Commission of, 70
  White Fish Authority of, 78
Great South Channel, 132
Greece, fishery of, 138
Greenland:
  cod fishery of, 82-83, 171
  East, Current, 121
  economic importance of fisheries
    of, 151-152
  West, 143
Grimm, Jacob, 18
Grimm, Wilhelm, 18
Gulf of St. Lawrence, 137

Gulf of Maine, 32
Gulf Stream, 121, 157
Gulland, J. A., 36
gulls, as bait for cod, 6

haddock:
  eggs, 24, 165
  fishery, 2, 4, 38, 45-46, 135, 136, 167
  minimum catch size of, 169
  research on, population, 170-173
    passim
  trawling for, 149, 160
hagdons, as bait for cod, 6
hake, 4, 135, 169
  Atlantic, 46
  luminous, 37
  Pacific, 46
  red, 47-48, 146
  silver, 46-47, 146
  white, 47
halibut, 122, 148, 149
Hamlisch, R., 62
Hammerle, O. A., 5
Hanseatic League of northern Europe, 14, 57
Hansen, Paul M., 32, 151
Hardy, Sir Alister, 24
Harland, James R., 48
hatch-boats, 70-71
hatcheries, 22, 154, 164-166
Havundersokelser Fiskeridirekto-
  ratets, 158
Hawkins, Sir John, 94
Helen H. II, 141
Helluland, *see* Labrador
Hennemuth, Richard C., 137
Henry IV, Part I (Shakespeare), 11
herring, 1, 24, 28
  as bait for cod, 6
  commercial landings of, 50
  fishery, 53-54, 146-148 *passim*
  salt, 5, 10, 53
Herrington, William C., 168
Hey, Joseph, 74-75, 78
*Hidden Treasures, or Fisheries
  Around the Northwest* (McDon-
  ald), 41-42
Hilditch, T. P., 58
Hjort, Johan, 158
Holt, Ernest W. L., 160-161
Houk, Richard J., 84

Hungary, National Museum of, 51
Huxley, Thomas, 155, 161
Hyperia, 26

ice, for preservation of fish, 71, 73
Iceland:
cod fishery of, 4, 138, 143, 147
per capita consumption of fish in, 65
stockfish markets of, 47, 63-64
Vikings in, 83
ICNAF, *see* International Commission for the Northwest Atlantic Fisheries
Idyll, C. P., 84
Innis, Harold A., 89
Institute of Marine and Atmospheric Sciences, 84
International Commission for the Northwest Atlantic Fisheries (ICNAF), 46, 168, 170
International Council for the Exploration of the Sea (ICES), 156, 168-169
International Game Fish Association, 30, 140
Iowa State Conservation Commission, 48
Ipswich (Mass.), 125
Irish Sea cod, 32
Iron Curtain countries, fishery of, 40, 43, 46, 47, 49-50, 78-79, 137-138, 144-146
Irwin, Richard W., 13

Jamaica, 140
Japan, cod fishery of, 40, 44, 138
Jeffreys Ledge, 90
jellyfish, red, 25-26
Jess-Lu III, 138
jigging, 28, 113, 148
Johan Hjort, 158, 159
Jordan, David S., 43
Journal (Winthrop), 94-95

Kay, Samuel, 58
Kipling, Rudyard, 8, 117-120
Kingston Peridot, sinking of, 76

Labrador:
cod fishery of, 112, 143, 146

Labrador (*cont.*)
Current, 121
discovery of, by the Vikings, 82
Lake Mogilno, 39
Lake Oppegaard, 71-72
lawyer, *see* burbot
Lea, Einer, 33
Leatherstocking Tales (Cooper), 12
Lindsay, Estele, 31
line trawl, fishing with, 31, 116-117, 119, 124
ling (*see also* burbot)
European, 47
lingcod, 49
Linnaeus, Carolus, 37
lobsters, 27
Lofoten Islands cod fishery, 4, 24, 25, 33, 54, 124, 138, 143, 156-157, 159
long-line fishery, 71

McCallum, E. V., 59
Macaulay, Franklin, 59
McCracken, Frank D., 33
McDonald, J. L., 41-42
McFarland, Raymond, 113-115
McHugh, J. L., 163
McKenzie, R. A., 35, 43
mackerel, 46
Mannix, Daniel, 100, 103
Marak, Robert R., 24, 25
Marblehead (Mass.), 89, 90
Mar Caribe, 150
Marine Sciences Center, of McGill University, 44
Marine Sciences Research Center, at Stony Brook, N. Y., 163
Marjorie Parker, 124
Markland, *see* Newfoundland
Martin, W. R., 149
Massachusetts:
Commission on Fisheries and Game, 130, 167
House of Representatives, cod in, 9, 12-13
Massachusetts Bay colony, 89, 162
Mayflower, 88
meal, fish, 50
menhaden, 28, 50
mercury, effect of, on fish, 152
Merluccius, 46-47
Mexico, cod fishery of, 150-151

Miller, David, 24
Miller, Morton, 131
mine fish, 47
Montauk (N. Y.), 31, 126, 139
moonsnail, 27
Murphy, Robert C., 3-4
Museum of Natural History, 3-4

Nantucket Shoals, 30, 34, 90
Nashe, Thomas, 56-57
Nature, 36
Nelson, S., 60
nets:
  gill, 124-125, 142
  pound, 163
  trawl, 72, 156, 160-161, 169, 170-171
New Bedford (Mass.), as scallop port, 27
Newburyport (Mass.), 31, 140
New England:
  fisheries of, 5, 27, 86-91 *passim*, 96, 109-111
  Golden Triangle of, 93-104
  revolution in fishing gear of, 124-125
New England Marine Resources Information Program, 11
Newfoundland (*see also* Grand Bank)
  and economics of the cod fisheries, 144
  settlement of, 85
  Vikings in, 82
News of Norway, 44, 147
New Jersey, cod fishery of, 33, 34, 138-139
Newport (R. I.), rum distilling in, 93, 102
Newton, Captain John, 99-100
New York State Division of Marine and Coastal Resources, 152
New York Times, The, 121-122
Nielsen, Adolph, 22
North America, development of domestic cod fishery of, 5-6
North American Council on Fishery Investigations (NACFI), 166
North Atlantic:
  cod fishery of, 3, 143-153
  Current, 157
Northeast Atlantic Fisheries Convention (NEAFC), 169-170, 172

North Carolina, Outer banks of, 4, 6
North Sea, trawl fishery of, 58
Norton, Virgil, 131
Norway:
  Biological Station at Trondheim, 22
  cod fishery of, 4, 24, 25, 33, 54, 124, 138, 143, 156-157, 159
  and economics of cod fisheries, 147
  Fisheries Directorate of, 147
  fish population studies by, 156-160, 172

Ocean Science Laboratory, N. Y., 152
oil, fish, 50, 54, 57-59
Olsen, John G., Jr., 112
otter trawl, 66, 126, 127-129, 148, 160, 167, 170

Pacific Ocean, fishery in, 40-41, 44-45
Pariser, E. R., 5
Pastore, Marty, 31
Patriarch Cod, 31
Peabody Museum, 91
Peconic Queen, 139
pelecypods, 27
perch, ocean, *see* redfish
Percidae, 49
Perley, M. H., 116
Petersen, C. G. J., 32
photography, deep water, 159
Pickman, Benjamin, 91
Pilgrims, 89-90
Playa de la Concha, 149
Plymouth colony, establishment of, 88, 89
Plymouth Land Company, 13
Poland, cod fishery of, 78-79, 137-138, 145, 146
Polańska, Aurelia, 78
pollock, 4, 27, 44, 165
  Alaska, 44
  walleye, 44
Pope, Alexander, 15
Pope Paul VI, 11
Porter, Jay, 138-139
Portland (Maine), 125
Portugal, cod fishery of, 4, 84-85, 90, 148
Prace Morskiego Instytutu Rybackiego, 78

Price, Tom, 122-123
Pring, Martin, 87

Quest of the Schooner Argus, The (Villiers), 148

Rainbowe, 95
Rasmussen, Hallstein, 147-148, 172
redfish, 49
"red tide," 172
Relation of the Fisheries to the Discovery and Settlement of North America (Woodbury), 91-92
religion, relationship between fish and, 1, 5, 9-11, 18-19, 54, 55, 65, 144
Report of Practical and Scientific Investigations of the Cod Fisheries near the Loffoden Islands (Sars), 157
Revere, Paul, 14
Revolutionary War:
contributing factors to the beginning of, 105
impact of, on New England cod fishery, 109-111
Rhodes, Samuel, 97-99
Roberts, Ernest W., 13
rockfish, *see* cod, rock
Rodway, James, 107
Rollefsen, Gunnar, 22-24, 158-159
Ross Cleveland, sinking of, 76-77
Ross Orion, 75, 77
Rostock Fisheries Combines, 146
rum (*see also* Golden Triangle, The), distillation of, 93, 102-104

Sabine, Lorenzo, 113, 135
sablefish, 49
Sable Island, 121
St. Andrews Biological Station, 35
St. George's Bank, *see* Georges Bank
St. Martin, Alexis, 60-61
St. Romanus, sinking of, 76
saithe, *see* pollock
Salem (Mass.), 90, 91, 101
Gazette, 14
salmon, 51
salt (*see also* cod, dried salt), manufacture of, 68-70, 85
Sars, G. O., 24-26, 157-158

scallop, deep-sea, 27
schooner, dory fishing from, x, 116-124
Schroeder, William C., 33, 34, 48, 166
Scorpaenidae, 49
Scotland:
Fishery Board of, 160
scup, 163
sea bass, 163
sea clam, 27
Sea Fisheries Institute, 78
Seafreeze Atlantic, 133-134
seal, fur, 44
Shakespeare, William, 1, 11
Sheepshead Bay Cod and Whiting Tournament, 141
Shetland Islands, crofters in, 69-70
shrimp, 27
skate, 149
Skazochnik Andersen, 50
slaves, *see* Golden Triangle, The
Smith, Captain John, 5, 87-88
Smith, Hugh M., 32, 125
sounding lead, 117-118
South Africa, hake fishery of, 38, 47
South America, demand for salt cod in, 63
South Korea, cod fishery of, 40, 45
Spain, fisheries of, 63, 90, 137, 149-151
Speaker, Everett B., 48
Spitzbergen-Bear Island, 143
Spray, 128
squid, 6, 28, 29, 148
Stansby, Maurice E., 59
stockfish, 47, 54, 57, 62-63, 67, 147
Sweden, Department of Fisheries of, 152
swordfish, banning sale of, 152
syphilis, 86

tautog, 163
Taylor, C. C., 31
Taylor, R. A., 62
television, underwater (UTV), 159-160
Three Brides, Love in a Cottage and Other Tales (Durivage), 12
Thomas Whalen, 133
tomcod:
Atlantic, 48-49
Pacific, 48-49

trawlers, 33
  beam, 160
  the fishermen of, 127-138 *passim*
  fishing by pairs of, 149-151
  otter, 66, 126, 127-129, 148, 149, 160,
    167, 170
trawl nets, 72, 156, 160-161, 169, 170-
  171
Trinity Bay, cod hatchery at, 22
Trout, Geoffrey, 33-34
trout, spawning of, 21
Tusser, Thomas, 10

Uhland, Hugo, 139
underwater television, 170
Union of Soviet Socialist Republics:
  Antarctic fishery of, 49-50
  cod fishery of, 40, 43, 66, 137-138,
    142, 145-146, 154
  exploitation of haddock stocks by,
    46
  exploitation of hake stocks by, 47
  Northern Fisheries Administration
    of, 50
United Nations:
  Food and Agriculture Organiza-
    tion of, 62
  World Food Program of, 144
United States, 30
United States:
  Bureau of Commercial Fisheries,
    10-11, 31, 47-48, 59, 60, 130, 131,
    150, 165, 166, 167
  Bureau of Fisheries, 32
  Commission of Fish and Fisheries,
    40, 43, 117, 124, 125, 157, 162-164
  Congress of, and salt cod trade, 111
  Department of Commerce, 3
  fishery studies of, 162-173 *passim*
  Food and Drug Administration
    (FDA), 152
  market for cod from, 64-65, 144
  National Marine Fisheries Service,
    2, 5, 49

United States (*cont.*)
  per capita fish consumption in, 65
  Pharmacopoeia (USP), 59
Ural, 142

Viking, 31
Vikings, explorations of, 1, 5, 82
Villiers, Alan, 96, 104, 148
Vineyard Sound, 86-87
Vinland, settlement of, 82-83
Vodnyi Transport, 43, 49-50

Waldo, Samuel, 97-98
Walters, Angus, 74
water temperature:
  effect of, on cod migration, 34
  and growth rate of fish, 23, 25, 30
  and spawning cod, 23, 25, 35
Weeden, W. B., 103
well-boats, 70-72
Wenham Lake ice, 71-72
West Spitzbergen Current, 34
whelks, 71
Whitbourn, Richard, 7
Whitehill, Walter Muir, 89, 91
whiting:
  blue, 47
  European, 47
  pout, 47
Whur, George J. D. T., 75, 77, 78
Williamson, G. R., 36
Winthrop, John, 88, 89-90, 94-95
Wise, John P., 2, 32-36 *passim*
wolffish, 148
Woodbury, C. L., 91-92
Woods Hole (Mass.):
  Albatross III of, 44, 59
  Albatross IV of, 137
  fish hatchery at, 154, 164, 165
  research conducted at, 2, 24, 33,
    45, 48, 163–166 *passim*
World Fishing, 78